ELEMENTS
OF LEADERS
OF
CHARACTER

ATTRIBUTES, PRACTICES, AND PRINCIPLES

Introduction to leaders of character and character-based leadership development

WAYNE HOGUE

WESTBOW
PRESS
A DIVISION OF THOMAS NELSON

WestBow Press books may be ordered through booksellers or by contacting:

WestBow Press
A Division of Thomas Nelson
1663 Liberty Drive
Bloomington, IN 47403
www.westbowpress.com
1-(866) 928-1240

Because of the dynamic nature of the Internet, any web addresses or links contained in this book may have changed since publication and may no longer be valid. The views expressed in this work are solely those of the author and do not necessarily reflect the views of the publisher, and the publisher hereby disclaims any responsibility for them.

Any people depicted in stock imagery provided by Thinkstock are models, and such images are being used for illustrative purposes only.

Certain stock imagery © Thinkstock.

ISBN: 978-1-4908-0343-2 (sc)
ISBN: 978-1-4908-0342-5 (hc)
ISBN: 978-1-4908-0344-9 (e)

Library of Congress Control Number: 2013913948

Printed in the United States of America.

WestBow Press rev. date: 8/06/2013

Table of Contents

Introduction

How would you like to make the world a better place while also improving every aspect of your own life and future?

Yes? Good! Keep reading. There are some people out there right now working hard every day to make the world a better place while also dramatically improving their own lives and the lives of everyone they impact. This book is a comprehensive examination of these people, written so that anyone can adopt the same attributes, practices, and principles into his or her own life in also becoming one of these people.

More than six years went into writing this book, and amazingly, the only certainty is it will never really be finished—the science discussed herein is young, vast, complicated, and dynamic. The original intent was to create an introduction to leadership textbook for a college class because there seemed to be few books that simplified the subject of leadership in a way conducive to introducing the topic to young people who may have never been introduced to the idea before. The thousands of hours spent on this work has shown why: leadership is an extremely abstract, complex, and intangible concept, and it is so different for each leader and in each situation, especially longitudinally over time and experience, so it is nearly impossible to simplify.

Through the research and writing process, the conclusion was made that though the act or skill of leadership may be difficult to teach, helping and guiding others to develop into the kind of person the world needs learning leadership, and out there leading, would be the greatest goal this book could pursue. With the endless stream of disgraced leaders, managers, athletes, and politicians that we are subjected to in the news almost daily, for the sake of our world this book will go a step further in creating the kind of leaders who lead for the right reasons. These are leaders who are disgusted by disgraced leaders and want to make things better; the leaders the world needs right now: leaders of character.

Many brilliant people have looked under the hood of leadership and given the world their interpretation—this book is another. No interpretation is final, but each advances the science of leadership a little further. Numerous quotes from many of these brilliant people spanning thousands of years of human history are used in this book. Significant thought and effort went into making sure every quote supports an important point being made. If Abe Lincoln, Gandhi, or Aristotle said something that is still pertinent today and supports a point being made, it is likely a point that we should all pay attention to.

It will be obvious as you read that the United States military and their service academies had considerable influence on this book. The military has long known the value of leadership; nobody goes to such lengths or has been developing leaders and teaching leadership longer. In the process of studying military leadership development, the elevated level of honor, pride, professionalism, respect, and sense of duty inherent in the military culture and most military personnel produced the epiphany that if even a small portion of that intrinsic ethic could be captured and transferred to the civilian population, the result could be positively transforming on society. If we inflate the value of character in society the way the military has done it, we will have a phenomenal impact on our world—that is what leaders of character do.

While the elements are listed as individual components here, they are actually extremely interrelated pieces of very complex and complicated entities (leaders of character). This book is an effort to simplify the complexity somewhat and offer an understandable compilation or inventory of the more important and most noted attributes, practices, and principles. Being an introductory book, barely the tip of most of the concepts and ideas is discussed in this book so you will determine for yourself which concepts to drill down into further. To aid in follow-on research, a listing of numerous leadership (or related) books is offered in the appendix at the back of the book.

This is not a character development book per se, but character is certainly a major focus. A major difficulty in writing about character is it is even more abstract, complex, expansive, and more of a mystery than leadership. The difficulty is most notable in the search for satisfactory words or verbiage to precisely and accurately categorize, describe, define, or label many of the concepts and ideas. When no single word or phrase exists that accurately conveys the intended meaning of a concept or term, a string of labels or descriptors must be used to narrow in on the intended description or meaning. With a general idea of the concept, further clarity will come through subsequent discussions. So, when a string of optional descriptions or words are used in defining a concept, it is because the precisely desired verbiage does not exist.

Being a leader or a person of character is very hard because it is difficult to live by the principles in this book. There are considerable forces and distractions in today's world that seem to steer us away from living a life of character. It might appear that the world does not value the doctrine this book is based on; however, leaders must be concerned about where our families, communities, and society are headed if society does not start putting an emphasis and value on character. The valuation of character has to start somewhere—why not now, why not here, and why not with us?

By the end of this book, all of the ideals and principles herein will be brought home and made personal to you, to every reader. By the end of this book, you will know just how intricately this applies to your life, and then, the conclusion will spell how valuable this book is to you and your life. But you cannot just skip ahead; everything between here and the end is what makes it true.

So let us begin.

SECTION 1

Leaders, Leadership, Character, Character-Based Leadership, and Leaders of Character

CHAPTER 1

Elements of Leaders of Character

Our world is changing at breakneck speed, and while much of our daily lives is becoming more and more about automation, autonomy, convenience, speed, and technology, one thing has not, and never will change: humans are social beings who need to interact socially with others. In this rampant change, it seems that many of the "old-timey" traditional family, hard work, self-supporting, and faith or virtue-based values that once helped guide civilized society's culture made way for a more relaxed, casual, and (many believe) much less wholesome and robust culture. This new culture has advanced society in many ways, but it has had some detrimental effects as well.

The culture of any society (as well as countries, communities, groups, organizations, and even families) is determined by the kind of people who make up the society. Therefore, in response to some of the detrimental cultural trends, there is an emerging (or reemerging) focus and concern on identifying the kind of people who positively advance society, discovering what it is about them that makes them the kind of people they are, and then introducing those attributes, practices, and principles back into the population in the hopes of developing more of that kind of person. This concern is not only for the betterment of society itself, but perhaps even the very future of civilized society because the most important factor in the rise and decline of societies is the character of the people who form that society. The strategy is this: a person's character defines the kind of person he or she is, so improve the character of the people in a society and thereby improve society. This focus is also bringing attention to the absolutely critical role character plays in every aspect of a person's life.

One example of the new focus is the discussion taking place on teaching character development in school (elementary, high school, and college) in conjunction with the traditional subjects and skills. The reality is becoming clearer that the abysmal educational dropout rate and resultant decimating social problems are much more about the character of the students, friends, and parents than they are about anything to do with the schools. The new thinking is to focus on developing the character of the kids in school so that they will become better students and the kind of people who understand the value of education and the incredibly positive impact education has on their lives, community, and country. Develop the character of the people, and all of society's problems will begin to decrease.

Great idea!

Thankfully, there are already some great role models that we can learn about character from because it defines who they are and what they do. These role models are *leaders of character*, the subject of this book.

Elements of Leaders of Character—attributes, practices, and principles of leaders who value strong, positive, virtuous character—is a leadership book, but more specifically it is a leader development book. It is a textbook that serves as an introduction to the subjects of leaders of character and character-based leadership. Most importantly, it is a book about self-improvement through character development.

The primary goal of *Elements of Leaders of Character* is to promote development of more leaders of character by detailing the adoptable and developable elements (attributes, practices, and principles) that exemplify this kind of leader. This book is a comprehensive illustration and discussion of many of the components of leaders who value their good solid character and live their lives accordingly.

The *elements* are the basic foundational aspects of leaders of character. They include

> *Attributes*: characteristics, descriptions, traits, ingredients, components
> *Practices*: behaviors, actions, skills, habits, activities
> *Principles*: beliefs, qualities, ideals, standards, values

Leaders of character are leaders who lead for the right reasons. They are people who place the highest value on good, strong, positive character because they fully know the impact of their character on their leadership and their lives. Leaders of character genuinely care about becoming better people and leaders in order to make a positive impact on the world. People, especially groups of people, naturally want and need someone to lead, to set a direction to head or an example to follow. A leader's character is what determines his or her direction or example.

It will become obvious in the following pages that teaching or learning leadership is difficult because of the abstractness and ambiguity of the act or skill of leadership. Leadership cannot be learned from a single book. However, learning how to become a person of character is not as difficult since our character is comprised of a multitude of malleable and dynamic elements that can be intentionally positively developed.

So let's begin with some good, clear descriptions to develop a common understanding.

CHAPTER 2

Leader and Leadership—Superstars

Leadership is like a rock star these days; it is everywhere. Leadership books, classes, conferences, consultants, DVDs, gurus, seminars, speakers, and workshops abound the land, and the words *leader* and *leadership* are used extensively in abundant and assorted contexts and connotations. These days we all know leadership is important, and everyone probably has an idea of what it is, but it is still a safe bet that if we asked a hundred people to define *leader* and *leadership*, a hundred different variations and definitions would likely result. So, with such widespread notoriety, how could there be such confusion over superstar words and concepts as popular as *leader* and *leadership*?

There is no single answer to the question, but the authors of the book *Made to Stick*,[1] Chip and Dan Heath, introduced a concept they called "semantic stretch" that diagnoses one part of the problem in the lack of a general clarity of what leadership really is. Semantic stretch is the phenomenon where words and concepts and their true meaning become diluted and changed through overuse and/or consistent misuse. For example, the Heaths researched the historical use of the words *unique*

---

[1] Heath, Chip and Dan Heath. *Made to Stick*. New York City: Random House Publishing Group. 2007. Print.

and *unusual* by newspaper reporters and found that the use of *unique* has significantly increased and the use of *unusual* has decreased because *unique* has more "emotional kick" in a news story. Something that is unique is much more interesting than something that is unusual. The result is the meaning of the word *unique* has lost much of its clarity through the overuse and misuse. The same phenomenon has engulfed *leader* and *leadership* as well, causing some of the lack of clarity or misunderstanding of what they really are.

The issue driving the overuse and misuse of the words *leader* and *leadership* is that the words add clout, credibility, or authority to whatever they are attached to. News reporters and writers regularly use both words because they automatically increase credibility of any news report or story. When inserted into the title of a book, program, or article, these words increase significance and clout automatically (regardless of the content). When *leader* is used to describe a person or a job, that person instantly becomes more of an authority and more credible (regardless of their true credibility). Writers, reporters, and even higher education and industry have all contributed to the confusion and semantic stretch of the words because *leader* and *leadership* are regularly used in place of

- *manager* and *management* in business;
- *officer/commander* and *command* in the military and military education;
- *principal/administrator* and *administration* in education;
- *pastor* or *church management* in theology; and
- *politician* and *governing/government management* in the context of politics.

Truthfully, all of the jobs and activities listed above are actually managers and management. Therefore, in deciphering leadership, we will proceed by comparing it to generic management, keeping in mind that we are talking about all of them. Comparing and contrasting management and leadership is a great way to clear up some of the confusion over leadership and illustrate exactly what it is and what it is not. Most people have some understanding of what management is; therefore, it makes a good comparative example.

CHAPTER 3

Management vs. Leadership

Leadership is often thought of as a business function because many people think leadership and management are the same thing. This belief was so widespread in the past that many university leadership programs were developed and housed in the business school and leadership classes were taught by business management professors. This business school mixing of management and leadership only added to the confusion of understanding leadership and furthered the semantic stretch of the words *leader* and *leadership*. Now that it is widely understood that leadership is not the domain of business or management but is instead a social science inclusive to everyone from every walk of life, university leadership programs are scattered throughout the campus. However, the mingling of management and leadership is still widespread, and they are synergistic functions, so comparing and contrasting the two offers a great way to illustrate leadership.

The similarity between management and leadership that drives the intertwining of the words is they both involve an interaction between people: superiors and subordinates in management; leaders and followers in leadership. Furthering the similarity, there can also be a social aspect to management and a management aspect to leadership. However, the two are separate and independent actions or functions wherein management is mostly a business function or process, and leadership is mostly a personal interaction. The leader and manager can certainly be the same person, but the manager in a business is not necessarily the leader, and the leader is not necessarily the manager. In fact, in many real-life workplace or organizational settings, the manager and the true leader are two different people.

Management is about doing; leadership is about being.

One issue clouding the difference between management and leadership is that much of what is said and written about leadership is penned by successful veteran managers (or management teachers, professors, consultants, etc.) who view leadership through a business management lens or paradigm. Management and leadership certainly do become increasingly intertwined over a successful long career with increasing levels of responsibility and authority, so it is easy to understand how the two functions meld together at some level in a successful manager's career. When managers reach executive level positions, they are very far removed from actual production so they must work through many other people to get things done. Since they spend their days working through and with people, leadership skills become increasingly valuable and intertwined with their success. Therefore, successful senior managers are likely to argue that management and leadership are the same thing.

Fittingly, for managers ambitious to enter higher levels of management, there could be no better guide and teacher than someone with lots of experience and success in high-level management; however, introductory-level learners (the majority of us) need a less complex and intertwined-with-management view of leadership. Additionally, exceptionally experienced people with vast knowledge in any area tend to have a very difficult time explaining concepts on an introductory level (the smartest and most experienced people often make the worst teachers). Leadership and management to a manager with thirty years of experience are vastly different than to a twenty-year-old college student. Early on, both management and leadership are much less complicated and significantly less intertwined.

Leadership to a young person is very different and far from management than it is to a seasoned manager or leader who may not see the difference at all anymore.

A common textbook definition of management is "reaching the goals and objectives of the organization by using assets and resources effectively and efficiently." Assets and resources include capital, equipment, raw materials, and employees. Managers are empowered (and paid) to decide how to best use the assets and resources at their disposal to reach their goals and objectives. To accomplish this, managers must have almost total control and authority over the business processes, including employees, in order to get the most out of the assets and resources. In other words, management is about control. Leadership, on the other hand, is not about control at all. It is more about empowering others and soliciting their free will and inner drive or spirit. Leadership is more about people, where management is more about processes, resources, and objectives. The following quote alludes to leadership's higher order contribution.

> Leadership is the art of accomplishing more than the
> science of management says is possible.
> —General Colin Powell, American statesman and
> retired four-star Army general

Leadership empowers people's free will to do more than management control can.

The following observations from Warren Bennis, one of the pioneers of modern leadership thought, shed more light on differences between managers and leaders:

> The manager accepts the status quo; the leader
> challenges it. …
> The manager asks how and when; the leader asks
> what and why. …
> The manager has a short-range view; the leader has a
> long-range perspective. …
> The manager has his eye on the bottom line; the
> leader has his eye on the horizon. …
> Leaders are people who do the right thing; managers
> are people who do things right. …
> —Warren G. Bennis, pioneer in the contemporary
> field of leadership studies

Management also differs from leadership in that it is quantifiable and measureable where leadership is not so much. Managers rely heavily upon metrics to make decisions and determine how and where to use resources, people, and assets. Progress is tracked, and success or failure is determined by the numbers (profits, productivity, costs, return, etc.). Quantification also means employees are retained (or not) based on whether they benefit the organization more than they cost, and a manager's competency is evaluated on their numbers—when the head office calls to check on things, they are not calling to check on the manager's health, they are calling to check on the numbers. Conversely, little about leadership can be measured, gauged, charted, or judged. In fact, the effects of leadership may never even be seen since there are no metrics with which to benchmark it.

Both management and leadership are ultimately about a person having some kind of power over, upon, or with others. The definition of *power* in this context is "the capacity to exert influence over others." Managers are assigned power from their bosses, whereas leaders are given power by the people they influence. A manager's power is based mostly on the authority of his or her position or job title; a leader's power comes mostly from the kind of leader and person he or she is. Manager's primary powers include

- *legitimate power* (based on title, position, or rank);
- *reward power* (ability to provide rewards or payment);
- *punishment power* (ability to penalize);
- *informational power* (ability to control information or knowledge that subordinates deem valuable); and
- *coercive power* (ability to make or force others to do something, even against their own will).

These managerial powers, while significant when in place, are very short-lived and completely dissipate as soon as the manager's authority vanishes. A manager has little power over subordinates outside of the official workplace.

A leader's primary powers include

- *referent power* (derived from personal relationships, trustworthiness, and character);
- *leadership power* (derived from stepping up when leadership is needed);
- *persuasion power* (derived from professional communications skills);
- *audacity power* (derived from boldness and daring);
- *charismatic power* (derived from personal likability, magnetism, and charm);
- *connectional power* (derived from personal relationships and associations with other leaders and influential people); and
- *expert power* (derived from professionalism, credibility, and expertise).

Because a leader's powers are based upon the kind of person a leader is, the powers transcend titles, authority, and the workplace. A leader's powers far surpass a manager's powers in strength and longevity, which is one of the primary reasons for the increasing intermingling of management and leadership throughout a management career. Successful managers learn and tap into the incredible benefits of both powers.

A boss creates fear, a leader confidence. A boss fixes blame, a leader corrects mistakes. A boss knows all, a leader asks questions. A boss makes work drudgery,

a leader makes it interesting. A boss is interested in
himself or herself, a leader is interested in the group.
—Russell H. Ewing, British journalist and author

While management (including command, administration, governing,
etc.) and leadership are certainly connected and synergistic, it is clear
that they are separate individual functions and actions. In learning
leadership, it must be thought of like any other skill on a sort of scale
where early on it is less complicated, but as we progress and advance,
it will become more complicated and intermingled with many other
actions, duties, and skills.

With this introductory-level focus, we drill down to the very essence
of leadership and not look at it on such a lofty level as if from a long-
tenured leadership/management position. We have to bring it down
to its most simple level. While we might not be able to decipher a
description or definition that is completely applicable to every leadership
situation, a clear and simple definition of *leader* and *leadership* that
anyone can adopt is certainly needed for our purposes here.

CHAPTER 4

Simple Concrete Definition of Leader and Leadership

Leader is easy to define and identify: he or she is the individual who offers or dispenses leadership. The leader is the person who gets other people to act or do something; he or she sets the direction or the example for others to follow.

Leadership, on the other hand, is the intangible force that leaders wield that causes followers to act, do something, head in the intended direction, or follow the leader's example. Leadership literally takes place in the sublime interaction between a leader and each individual person he or she affects. While many people may be simultaneously impacted by a single leader, each person or follower is individually impacted irrespective of anyone else. One irrefutable truth is that leadership takes place exclusively between two people: a leader and a follower.

Leadership is a social science; it is about interactions and relationships between people—human interactions— between a leader and a follower.

So to truly define leadership, we have to define the intangible force that causes followers to act. To do that, we can go to something one of the greatest leadership gurus of all time said. John Maxwell wrote in *The 21 Irrefutable Laws of Leadership*[2] (probably the number one leadership book on the planet) that "the measure of leadership is influence, nothing more, nothing less." If leadership, the intangible force that causes followers to act, is measured by influence, and leadership is about the leader influencing others, the simple concrete definition of leadership we need becomes very apparent.

The simple definition of leadership is *influence.* Accordingly, the simple definition of *leader* is "*the person who influences others or followers.*"

Leaders influence others to act, go a certain direction, or follow the leader's example; therefore, the definition of leadership is simply "influence."

The dictionary[3] definition of *influence* is "the act or power to produce effects, actions, or behaviors without apparent exertion of force or direct exercise of command." Therefore, the long definition of leadership is then "the intangible power or ability to cause others to act or do something without the help of authority, title, or any physical means to force it to happen."

---

2   Maxwell, John C. *The 21 Irrefutable Laws of Leadership*. Nashville: Thomas Nelson. 2007. Print.

3   Merriam-Webster. http://www.merriam-webster.com/dictionary/influence. Web. 19 June 2013

Leadership is influence, the intangible force that leaders wield that moves others to act.

One of America's founding fathers supported this definition.

> If your actions inspire others to dream more, learn
> more, do more, and become more, you are a leader.
> —John Quincy Adams, sixth president of
> the United States

In other words, if your influence causes somebody else to do something (anything), you are leading. The real benefit of this simple concrete definition is it makes the topic of leadership accessible to everyone.

CHAPTER 5

Everyone Is Included

The great thing about this simple definition—influence—is it opens leadership up to just about everybody because everyone influences others on some level or in some way. Leadership is not reserved for the high profile, title-holding, minuscule percentage of the population who tend to be given the title of "leader." No, leadership is more about everyday people, but especially those who make the conscious choice to step up and intentionally influence.

Influence can be seen in everyday activities; for example, the cashier at the checkout and the waiter at the restaurant are influenced by how we treat them or speak to them. The teacher in the classroom, friends, coworkers, and even strangers that we barely have contact with are influenced by us just the same, all the time. We have the ability to influence everyone we come in contact with every day, and in fact, we can influence people we do not even have contact with simply by how we look, dress, and act. For instance, a white shirt and red tie with a suit has an impact, as does a nice dress, or jeans and an old T-shirt (albeit very different impacts). Each of these examples influences people differently, whether we actually have contact or not. The same goes for the car we drive, the house we live in, and even our friends who supply a ton of influential information about us to others. Make no mistake, we all influence.

> You don't have to be a "person of influence" to be
> influential. In fact, the most influential people in my
> life are probably not even aware of the things they've
> taught me.
> —Scott Adams, creator of the *Dilbert* comic strip

The power of role models illustrates the power of influence as well as the fact that influence does not rely solely on personal contact. Businesses have long known that people, especially young people, consistently dress and act like their role model (which can be good or bad). That is why companies pay celebrities so much to endorse a product; their endorsement will influence the people who admire them to purchase the product. That kind of influence can be on a monumental scale, but for everyday leaders, influence can also be as simple as just being the kind of person that others like and even discreetly emulate. Leaders intentionally take responsibility for the impact of their influence and make a conscious choice of what they want the result of their influence to be.

> Think twice before you speak, because your words
> and influence will plant the seed of either success or
> failure in the mind of another.
> —Napoleon Hill, personal success author

The power of influence is a monumental leadership responsibility.

Influence is the awesome power behind leadership, but this intangible force also adds to the abstractness of leadership.

CHAPTER 6

The Abstractness of Leadership

These conceptual definitions—"the intangible power that takes place in the sublime interaction between two people" and "the intangible power or ability to cause others to act or do something without the help of authority, title, or any physical means to force it to happen"—illustrate well the abstractness of leadership. *Abstract* means it cannot be easily seen, touched, manipulated, or measured. In comparison, subjects like biology, engineering, history, management, or math are much more concrete and tangible. Each of them can be seen, touched, manipulated, and measured where leadership cannot. This distinction between abstract and concrete subjects adds to the confusion and vague understanding people have of leadership. It also helps explain why academia has struggled to determine what to do with the subject and why no mass producible leadership recipe has been developed.

Adding to leadership's abstractness is that the strength of a leader's influence is never stationary. Instead, influence is continuously fluctuating, depending upon countless uncontrollable factors such as the situation, culture, simultaneous events, and the differences between people. Moreover, influence is extremely ambiguous in that it can affect each individual differently in every ever-changing situation. In fact, possibly the most telling indication of the abstractness of leadership is that we truthfully cannot even determine if influence is taking place at all at any given moment. About the only way to prove it exists is through its aftermath. All of this abstractness and ambiguity are prime factors in increasing the difficulty in teaching or even describing leadership. There should be little wonder why people spend their entire lives studying and trying to learn the art/science/skill of leadership, nor that there is still such confusion on leadership in the everyday population.

This examination of its abstractness and ambiguity also brings up an often asked question: Can leadership really be taught and learned? Yes—at least on some level and to some extent depending on the leader's commitment, opportunities, and situation. Of course, the best teacher by far is experience through trial and error (no big secret there). Many great leaders also have several experienced leaders as mentors and teachers throughout their leadership development who help guide them and offer sage advice along the way. All great leaders are also fanatical lifetime learners because loads of advice and real-world best practices are available in numerous media, especially books. The massive amount of information available today gives all leaders easy access to plenty of invaluable help and information that can be customized to fit most leadership situations or scenarios. A list of helpful leadership books is offered in the appendix at the back of this book.

Another similar question often asked is, Are leaders born or made? Leaders are absolutely made. More precisely, leaders make themselves. Of course, there are people born with more naturally developed elements or beneficial leadership traits or talents, but anyone can become a leader—our simple definition ("influence") insures this. In fact, even those who may be born with more natural talent for leadership must develop that talent or it will never be of benefit. The following two adamant quotes from two phenomenal leaders leave little room to question the assertion that leaders are made, not born.

> The most dangerous leadership myth is that leaders
> are born—that there is a genetic factor to leadership.
> This myth asserts that people simply either have
> certain charismatic qualities or not. That's nonsense;
> in fact, the opposite is true. Leaders are made rather
> than born.
> —Warren G. Bennis, pioneer of the contemporary
> field of leadership studies

> Leaders are made, they are not born. They are made
> by hard effort, which is the price which all of us must
> pay to achieve any goal that is worthwhile.
> —Vince Lombardi,
> legendary Green Bay Packers football coach

Leaders are not born or made—leaders make themselves!

While the act of leadership is clearly abstract and intangible, the person leading and what makes a leader are much more concrete and easier to describe and examine. In fact, to become great at the art/skill of leadership, it makes the most sense to first focus on becoming the kind of person who should be leading, then begin to develop your leadership (that is the main point of this book). A good way to start examining beneficial attributes, practices, and principles of leaders is to examine some of the great leaders from the past.

CHAPTER 7

Historical Leader Perspective

In our quest to develop a clearer idea of what a leader looks like, a good place to start is researching leaders from history. Following is a list of people from throughout the history of mankind, each of whom had a huge impact on lots of people and even the world. Much has been documented and written about them, their lives, and their leadership impact, so a lot can be learned from them.

Historical Leaders

Abraham Lincoln

Adolf Hitler

Attila the Hun

Augustus Caesar

Benito Mussolini

Benjamin Franklin

Catherine the Great

Crazy Horse

Diana, Princess of Wales

Eleanor Roosevelt

Florence Nightingale

Franklin Roosevelt

George Washington

James Madison

Jesus

Joan of Arc

John Adams

Joseph Stalin

Julius Caesar

Mahatma Gandhi

Mao Tse-tung

Margaret Thatcher

Martin Luther King Jr.

Mother Teresa

Napoleon Bonaparte	Teddy Roosevelt
Nelson Mandela	Thomas Jefferson
Pol Pot	Vladimir Lenin
Susan B. Anthony	Winston Churchill

Each of the individuals on this list influenced scores of people (some are still influencing millions today); several of them impacted the entire planet. Under our definition of leadership ("influence"), they were all definitely leaders. The introductory intent of this book precludes going into detail on each one; however, studying their well-documented lives and the impact of their influence is incredibly educational, instructional, and a good way to learn about leadership and leaders. The study of several on the list will also illustrate what not to do, which is just as important as knowing what to do. For instance, the most infamous and impactful person on the list, Adolf Hitler, wrote *Mein Kampf*[4], which gives a chilling insight into how he developed the power and influence that led to the deaths of millions. It is hard to read, but it is very eye-opening.

Most importantly for us, scanning the list illuminates something very obvious: some had a profoundly negative impact on the world and some had a profoundly positive impact. This stark divergence warrants examination.

---

[4] Hitler, Adolf. Mein Kampf. Ralph Manheim (Translator). New York. Reynal and Hitchcock. 1939. Print.

CHAPTER 8

Positive and Negative Impact Leaders

The names on the historical leader list could easily be ranked and placed individually on a continuum or scale ranging from the most negative impact to the most positive impact. With any knowledge of history, it is certainly easy to spot names on the list that had a horrendously negative impact on the world, and some who had a significantly positive impact based on their overall lifetime impact. Human nature being what it is, most of us likely know much more about the horrific people on the list than the virtuous people (bad news sells; good news does not). The value of this exercise is to learn what made them different and to examine the good and bad aspects of the two kinds of leaders. It is also a way for us to find historical role models that we can use to help guide our own leadership development.

While the leaders on the list did incredible things in their lifetimes, good and bad, it is important to acknowledge that they were also normal imperfect human beings, no different than any of us. We know the negative impact leaders were massively flawed, but the positive impact leaders were not perfect either.

The positive impact leaders also made mistakes (like all humans do). They probably made numerous poor choices in their lives, and they had moral lapses and indiscretions as well (some are well documented). Some were hated and even murdered, many broke the law openly, and some spurred social unrest that resulted in death and destruction. Yet, in spite of all their flaws, these leaders were still able to have an overall positive impact on the world over their lifetimes—just like the rest of us can do. In fact, perhaps the greatest benefit of studying imperfect historical leaders is in helping us realize our own imperfections can be overcome as well.

Adrift in the self-awareness of our own flaws and imperfections, encouragement and hope is found in the knowledge that even the greatest leaders in the history of the world had weaknesses, imperfections, and vices—just like us—and they overcame them just like we can.

In assessing the differences between the two groups of leaders on the list—negative versus positive lifetime impact—it is reasonable that the major difference between them could be boiled down to each one's character, or the kind of person each really was on the inside. The positive impact leaders possessed a more positive, compassionate, and virtuous character than the negative impact leaders. That is, each leader on the list had either a mostly stronger, more caring, positive, and virtuous character, or a mostly weaker, negative, and indifferent character as evidenced by their actions, what he or she did, and the impact he or she had. What they did to the world was a direct indication of the kind of people they were; their impact on the world was determined by their character.

Basing the determination of their character on their lifetime impact is actually categorizing them based on their character later in their lives when they were at the peak of their leadership and impact. While it is easy to determine where their character ended up, that does not mean that their character started out any different from one another at some early point in life. In fact, everyone starts out with the exact same character at birth; it is a blank slate that begins to develop as we become increasingly cognizant. If our character is a blank slate when we are born, it is an extremely safe assumption that we can also consciously determine or guide the development of our character and choose what we want it to be.

Before deciding what our character should be, we need to ask, What exactly is character?

CHAPTER 9

Character

Character is a combination, aggregate, or the sum of numerous components that form, define, and distinguish the kind of people we really are, on the inside (which also translates into the kind of people the outside world sees us as). Our character is our metaphysical self—everything about us except our physical, corporeal self. It is our soul, spirit, nature, psyche, and essence. Our character is the part of us that arrives before we arrive, and it stays after we leave.

The following quotes help clarify the metaphysical nature of character.

> The only thing that walks back from the tomb with
> the mourners and refuses to be buried is the character
> of a man. What a man is survives him. It can never be
> buried.
> —J. R. Miller, Christian pastor and author

> Character is like a tree and reputation like a shadow.
> The shadow is what we think of it; the tree is the real
> thing.
> —Abraham Lincoln, sixteenth president of the United
> States

Reputation is what men and women think of us;
character is what God and angels know of us.
—Thomas Paine, American founding father,
political activist, author

Character is who we actually are—the kind of people we truly are on the inside when all physical aspects and pretense are stripped away.

The study and mapping of character is a separate and much more daunting science than the study of leadership; however, the elements of leaders of character in this book are components or illustrators of character so an intense interest in character is critical. Character is completely intangible and internal, so it is studied by its outside-world interactions or factors that illustrate it to other people. *Outside-world* refers to behaviors, elements, or traits that others can see or experience that are illustrative of a person's character. The phrase "character strength" is used to refer to an outside-world trait that illustrates a desirable character trait, or a trait of someone with the kind of character that is beneficial to the person and society.

The science of character especially suffers from the lack of accurate words or verbiage necessary to exactingly explain or define various ideas within the science. The importance of the science is now reaching the radar of society, so there is a rapidly increasing public interest in character research, especially in terms of the benefits of character development and education in advancing society. In studying and discussing character, rather than focus on it as one immense unit, researchers and writers break it down into a number of related areas, segments, or categories illustrated by sets of specific outside-world character strengths, behaviors, elements, or traits. To match the purpose of this book, character can easily be broken down into four segments that are each correlated with several of the elements.

Moral Character: constitutes elements such as authenticity, compassion, honesty, honor, humility, integrity, morality, respect, sacrifice, trustworthiness, and values. Moral character is illustrated in how moral, honorable, and virtuously a person lives.

Performance Character: constitutes elements such as behavior, communication skills, competence, creativity, credibility, flexibility and adaptability, intuition, knowledge, people skills, professionalism, vision, and willingness to lead. Performance character is illustrated in how a person performs at tasks and duties such as at work, school, home, leadership, and in everyday life.

State-of-Mind Character: constitutes elements such as attitude, charisma, confidence, optimism, passion, and sense of humor. State-of-mind character is illustrated in how a person interacts with the world and other people moment by moment and over the long term.

Strength-of-Mind Character: constitutes elements such as commitment, courage, discipline, locus of control, perseverance, and responsibility and accountability. Strength-of-mind character is illustrated by the sturdiness, tenacity, and vitality of a person's mental or cognitive control and processes especially under duress or challenge.

It must be noted that the specific elements listed above constituting each segment of character are not really limited to that segment because most of the elements are important to more than one segment. For example, perseverance is an incredibly important *strength-of-mind* character strength; however, it is equally important to our *performance* of difficult tasks at work, school, etc., and it is significantly dependent upon our *state of mind* at any given moment as well, and it is fully required in maintaining *moral character*. Another example is attitude: it is an illustrator of our *state-of-mind character*; however, it is also illustrated by (and impacts) our *performance*. Our control over our attitude illustrates our *strength of mind*, and even how virtuously we act is heavily dependent upon our attitude.

Because character is the combination of multiple dynamic and ever-changing elements, character itself is also dynamic and ever-changing. We are conscious of significant changes in many of the elements, especially over time and throughout the different stages, ages, and chapters of life. Character's ever-changing status illustrates its most important aspect: if character is ever-changing, we have the ability to control and guide our own character's progress and development. Our character is a part of us that is never complete, so it is a lifelong process going on within us whether we are paying any attention to it or not.

The following quotes support the idea of lifelong character development.

Character isn't something you were born with and can't change, like your fingerprints. It's something you weren't born with and must take responsibility for forming.
—Jim Rohn, American entrepreneur, author, and motivational speaker

Character building begins in our infancy and continues until death.
—Eleanor Roosevelt, First Lady of the United States from 1933 to 1945

Good character is not formed in a week or a month. It is created little by little, day by day. Protracted and patient effort is needed to develop good character.
—Heraclitus (535-475 BC), pre-Socratic Greek philosopher

Character is one part of us that never stops changing—it is strengthening or weakening every day of our lives.

As we go through life, a multitude of factors and forces work to forge and mold our character. These forces include inherited physiological and mental factors, innate talents and traits, our upbringing (the way we are raised), friends and peer pressure, societal expectations and norms, culture, knowledge and experiences, good and bad events, choices and decisions we make, and countless other factors. This list of character development forces also supports the lifetime character development idea. The forces (and many more) are always impacting what kind of people we are.

Because of its abstractness, intangibility, and the impossibility of measuring it, determining the status of our character at any given moment is impossible. Though it has to be done on almost a conjectural level, self-monitoring is perhaps the only means to even remotely observe character. One hypothetical exercise to monitor or judge our own character development is to visualize or create a character development chart.

To be even more precise, an individual chart for specific segments of character can be created. The X axis (horizontal) will represent time (days, weeks, months, or years of life) and the Y axis (vertical) will represent the strength or measure of character. Dividing the Y axis in the middle horizontally will create a baseline hypothetical zero point. The area above the line represents stronger, more positive, and more virtuous character, and the area below the line represents weaker, more negative, and less virtuous character.

Throughout the stages, ages, and chapters of our day-to-day life, as we consciously watch our character develop, it could be plotted on the graph(s) creating an ever-changing line going from left to right. Live honestly, honorably, and remain trustworthy; build competence, credibility, and knowledge; maintain a great attitude, commitment, and perseverance; and the line will develop on the positive side of the hypothetical mean line. Live the opposite kind of life, and the line will drop to the negative side. While this may be just a hypothetical exercise, the important point is that by living a certain way (like living by the principles in this book), we can develop stronger, more positive, and more virtuous character. Of course, the opposite is also true.

It seems in today's world that negative character impacting forces are far more prevalent and resilient than positive forces. There have always been negative impact forces, but the casualization of society appears to be more accepting of those negative forces, so they appear to be much more open and pronounced these days. Regardless, the prevalence of these forces ensures that random character changes will likely be negative changes rather than positive changes. In other words, if we let our character develop unchecked, there is a good chance that it will not develop on the positive side of the character development chart.

This fact makes conscious intentional character development especially vital. Character development must be looked at as a lifelong self-improvement project with ups and downs, good and bad decisions, and right and wrong choices. The best strategy is simply to focus on steadily improving and accept the many difficulties and barriers that life throws at us as normal events—that is life. Leaders learn and grow from mistakes, misfortunes, missteps, and mishaps—in fact, these are some of our greatest teachers. We learn much more from losing or failing than from winning or succeeding. Leaders expect setbacks and use them as learning experiences.

> Faced with crisis, the man of character falls back on
> himself. He imposes his own stamp of action, takes
> responsibility for it, makes it his own.
> —Charles de Gaulle, French general, president,
> and statesman

Since personal relationships are critical for leaders, character's greatest importance and value is seen in its impact on every relationship in our lives. A strong, positive, virtuous, and caring character is perhaps the most potent relationship development and maintenance asset on the planet. To visualize this truth, simply think about what kind of relationships a person with weak, negative, evil, and uncaring character will have in their life!

Another fact about character is that no one can hide from their true character or the kind of person they really are. We simply cannot, for long, perform at a level far removed from who we really are or how we truly see ourselves in the mirror; our true character will eventually show. In the book *The Success Syndrome*,[5] Steve Berglas makes a point that people who achieve great heights but lack the solid character foundation to help them in handling the stress of achievement or position are likely to ultimately crash somewhere along the way. There have been many celebrity examples of this tragedy, but truthfully, it is likely that most people only achieve to the level of their character—character is the success limiter; the success ceiling. In other words, our level of success in everything we do in life will be determined by the strength of our character. Knowing this reality, leaders are extremely self-aware to avoid tragedy by developing the character to match their success.

Science may never fully map character; however, it is without a doubt a leader's (everyone's) greatest asset, strongest tool, and biggest lifetime

---

[5]   Berglass, Steven. *The Success Syndrome*. Boston, New York: Da Capo Press. 1986. Print.

project. We've illustrated the importance and malleability of character; now we need to tie it all together with leadership and leaders.

Character is like a light in a box. You cannot directly see it, but the beams shining through the cracks readily tell its quality and strength—the elements are those beams.

CHAPTER 10

Character-Based Leadership and Leaders of Character

Up to this point we have examined leaders, leadership, and character. Now, we will combine them.

Character-based leadership is constructive, positive, and virtuous influence. It is leadership that is not just setting any direction or example; it is setting a powerfully positive and beneficial direction or example. The long definition of character-based leadership is "the intangible power or ability to cause others to act or do something constructive, positive, or virtuous without the help of authority, title, or any physical means to force it to happen."

Character-based leadership is constructive, positive, and virtuous influence—the intangible force that leaders of character wield that moves others to act in beneficial and worthy ways.

Character-based leadership is about leading followers to cause beneficial and positive change. It is leadership with the best interests of everyone involved at heart while having a helpful and constructive impact on the world. Character-based leadership is leadership with nothing but good and honorable motives and intentions.

Character-based leadership is stepping up to lead—not to just lead, but to make the world a much better place.

Character-based leadership is leadership performed by leaders of character.

A *leader of character* is a person who has made a conscious decision to be the kind of person and leader who makes the world a better place. It is a person who has decided to intentionally look for opportunities to step up and lead, not just to be leading, but to cause positive change and to benefit others—to make things better. Leaders of character focus equal attention on developing their own character along with their leadership abilities. They enjoy being leaders because of the opportunity to positively influence others.

Leaders of character are people who are consciously intent on making a positive and constructive impact on other people and the world by being people and leaders with solidly strong, positive, and virtuous character.

The United States Air Force Academy's Center for Character and Leadership Development defines a leader of character[6] as a person who

---

[6] United States Air Force Academy Center for Character and Leadership Development. *Developing Leaders of Character.* Page 9. http://www.usafa.edu/Commandant/cwc/cwcs/docs/Flip_Books/CONCEPTUALFRAMEWORK27_OCT.pdf. Web. 19 June 2013

- Lives honorably by consistently practicing the virtues embodied in the Core Values of: Integrity First; Service before Self; and Excellence in All We Do.
- Lifts others to their best possible selves.
- Elevates performance toward a common and noble purpose of always better and always higher.

Aristotle, the famous Greek philosopher, suggested that a good leader (e.g., a leader of character) must have "ethos, pathos and logos." Truthfully, in ethos, pathos, and logos, Aristotle was talking about a leader's character, or more specifically three segments of character. Ethos (ethical), similar to moral character, is a leader's ability to create and maintain trust and respect with others. Pathos (feeling) is a leader's ability to touch feelings and move people on an emotional level; the leader must to be able to inspire others. Logos (logic) is a leader's ability to provide solid reasons for an action in order to move people intellectually; the leader must be knowledgeable and communicate well. A person who intensely valued ethos, pathos, and logos was the kind of leader needed in Aristotle's time—and it is still the kind of leader the world needs today.

A leader of character is a leader who intensively protects and develops ethos, pathos, and logos, along with moral, performance, state-of-mind, and strength-of-mind character, because all are vital.

Leaders of character may seem to be larger than life by these descriptions, but they are normal, everyday people who happen to live by an elevated set of values and principles. They can be found in every walk of life.

The behavior of leaders of character is not radical or over the top; most of their actions are common courtesy, usually by simply being a lady or gentleman. Following are a few examples of some everyday behaviors of leaders of character. They

- are ladies and gentlemen and treat others as ladies and gentlemen.
- maintain their standards, honor, integrity, trustworthiness, and values at all costs.
- accept responsibility and hold themselves accountable for the duties and responsibilities they accept.
- show everyone the respect and esteem deserved.
- readily give others credit for success and accept fault and blame for failures.
- volunteer; they are quick to help when possible.
- ask questions, because they understand the greatest subject on the planet is the person they are talking to.
- show genuine appreciation.
- think and care about the repercussions of actions.
- intensely value and appreciate honor.

Nothing on the list is difficult; however, maintaining these practices in the real world every day and in every situation is not easy. Most importantly, these behaviors are rarely rewarded or even noticed—that is just one price of being a leader of character.

So the question to ask now is, What is it about these people that make them leaders of character? The answer to this question is the following elements.

SECTION 2

The Elements of Leaders of Character

CHAPTER 11

The Elements

The *elements*—attributes, practices, and principles of leaders who value strong, positive, virtuous character—are a comprehensive, but far from complete picture, description, or inventory of many of the major aspects and traits, components, habits, activities, and quality-of-mind strengths that are common among leaders of character.

An element is one part of a complex whole; consequently, each of the elements listed here is an individual, but highly interrelated part of the very complex composition of a leader of character. The elements of leaders of character is the individual inventory of a complex interdependent system. Such complexity results in the number of components and the amount of information required to fully explain leaders of character to be excessive or almost too complicated a formula to be comprehended; however, leadership and leaders of character are just that complex, vast, and complicated—there is no shortcut. Actually, this book could be considered a short-cut because we only touch on the tips of the trees of the true amount of details and information possible herein. A detailed examination of each individual element could easily fill an entire book (or many books) on its own. So while the elements discussed here represent many of the more significant attributes, practices, and principles of leaders of character, they still only represent a portion of the total; but they do represent a good starting point for an introductory view.

The elements are the base or foundation in the development of a leader of character. Every leader and his or her world and situation is absolutely unique, requiring an exclusive set and variation of customized elements. Therefore, the elements will necessarily be personalized, customized, and tailored to fit each individual's specific circumstances. Furthering the difficulty, each individual leader must determine his or her own customization and variation; nobody can do it for us.

While we are not specifically seeking character development in this book, that is certainly an expected lagniappe effect. The goal of this book is to create more leaders of character, but there is a character development component in that goal. Fittingly, when character authors and researchers list major character traits, leadership is always on the list, so it could be said that this book focuses on a single character trait—leadership! The elements must be viewed in terms of leader development (rather than as character development) because the elements are aspects of leaders of character, what guides their leadership, their way of thinking, what leads them, what they do, how they act, what they value, and so forth. Because of the close relationship between the elements and character, the elements can also be divided into segments that directly correlate with the previously defined character segments. As with character, this segmentation helps in reducing the enormity and complexity of the overall scope of the elements. Note that the word *trait* is used (for lack of a better term) in place of *elements* or *attributes, practices, and principles* for the sake of simplicity.

- **Moral Traits:** includes authenticity, compassion, honesty, honor, humility, integrity, morality, respect, sacrifice, trustworthiness, and values. Moral traits illustrate how moral, honorable, and virtuous a leader of character is.

- **Performance Traits:** includes behavior, communication skills, competence, creativity, credibility, flexibility and adaptability, intuition, knowledge, people skills, professionalism, vision, and willingness to lead. Performance traits illustrate how a leader of character performs at tasks and duties such as at work, school, home, leadership, and in everyday life.

- **State-of-Mind Traits:** includes attitude, charisma, confidence, optimism, passion, and sense of humor. State-of-mind traits illustrate how a leader of character interacts with the world and other people moment by moment and over the long term.

- **Strength-of-Mind Traits:** includes commitment, courage, discipline, locus of control, perseverance, and responsibility and accountability. Strength-of-mind traits illustrate the sturdiness, tenacity, and vitality of a leader of character's mental or cognitive control and processes especially under duress or challenge.

One huge difficulty in a book on leaders of character is the problem that proper words or terminology do not exist to truly and accurately define and describe some of the elements and what they entail. This problem is magnified when including the discussion of the incredibly abstract character traits. In such cases, a list or stream of related or close words are used to attempt to narrow down the intended meaning or point. Hopefully the point will become clearer in the follow-on discussion.

So what are the attributes, practices, and principles that define leaders of character?

CHAPTER 12

Attitude

Attitude is a person's mental or emotional demeanor, disposition, temperament, posture or orientation toward others. It is viewed in a person's manner of acting or speaking that shows disposition, mood, opinion, or state of mind. It is the visible outward projection of state of mind or way of thinking. Attitude is how a leader interacts with others and the world.

Attitude is a state-of-mind trait because it is illustrative of a person's emotional, cognitive, and mental state. A state-of-mind trait is incredibly complex because of the number of factors, both internal and external, that impact it, such as our background, feelings, environment, genetics, mood, physical conditions, physiological conditions, well-being, and countless other factors. We have limited ability to consciously influence or control a state-of-mind trait like attitude, at least to a point, but because it is impacted by so many factors beyond our conscious understanding, complete control is impossible. Because so much of what impacts our state of mind is beyond our conscious understanding, the best, and perhaps only, strategy for leaders is a continuous focus on character development. Consequently, if we become stronger, more positive, and more virtuous people, our state of mind will also become stronger, more positive, and more virtuous.

> Attitude is more important than the past, than
> education, than money, than circumstances, than
> what people do or say. It is more important than
> appearance, giftedness, or skill.
> —W. C. Fields, American comedian, actor, and writer

One important aspect of attitude is our ability to consciously change it. Being human, strongly influenced by emotions, circumstance, physiology (i.e., hormones, etc.), and psychology, controlling or changing our attitudes may be difficult, but this is a skill or talent that can be learned and developed. The first step in controlling attitude is to develop control over emotions. Human emotions are extremely powerful, dreadfully volatile, and they change rapidly. Emotions cause people to do unbelievable things, both good and bad. Immeasurable harm and damage can be done when emotions take control of a person's thoughts and actions. It is likely that the majority of regret that many people shoulder can be traced to out-of-control of emotions; therefore, controlling emotions may be one of a leader's most important tasks.

Attitude is critical for leaders because the most basic essence of leadership is the personal one-on-one relationship between a leader and a follower and attitude is a significant determinant of the quality of all of our personal relationships. Bad attitudes lead to poor relationships and good attitudes elicit stronger relationships. Most important for leaders to remember is a sufficiently bad attitude can irreparably damage most any relationship.

> The only disability in life is a bad attitude.
> —Scott Hamilton, American figure skater and
> Olympic gold medalist

49

This passage from Charles Swindoll[7], an American pastor and author, does a great job of illustrating the importance of attitude.

> The longer I live, the more I realize the impact of attitude on life.
>
> Attitude, to me, is more important than facts. It is more important than the past, than education, than money, than circumstances, than failures, than successes, than what other people think or say or do. It is more important than appearance, giftedness or skill. It will make or break a company ... a church ... a home.
>
> The remarkable thing is we have a choice every day regarding the attitude we will embrace for that day. We cannot change our past ... we cannot change the fact that people will act in a certain way. We cannot change the inevitable. The only thing we can do is play on the one string we have, and that is our attitude ... I am convinced that life is 10% what happens to me and 90% how I react to it.
>
> And so it is with you ... we are in charge of our attitudes.

---

7   Swindoll, Charles R. http://thinkexist.com/quotes/charles_r._swindoll/. Web. 19 June 2013

Ninety percent of a leader's success in life is how he reacts to what life throws at him.

Further evidence of attitude's importance can be found in industry. It is said that employers rank attitude above talent in hiring decisions because they know they can train skills but they cannot train or fix a bad attitude. A popular saying and country song suggests the need for "an attitude adjustment." The phrase implies that a person's bad attitude needs to be forcefully and physically "improved." The phrase also signifies how much a bad attitude is detested, even to the possibility of using physical harm to change a bad attitude. Leaders must always keep in mind that there can rarely be a positive or constructive result or outcome from a negative, pessimistic, sour, arrogant, boastful, angry, or depressing attitude.

For leaders working on their character, the following quote from Albert Einstein highlights the direct connection attitude has with character.

> Weakness of attitude becomes weakness of character.
> —Albert Einstein, German theoretical physicist

Quality of attitude propagates quality of character.

So what should a leader of character's attitude be? Leaders endeavor to maintain an attitude that is

> *Attentive:* A leader must be attuned to followers and the surroundings—attention signals care and concern, which leaders must have and show.

Can-do: A leader has to be able to get things accomplished—if the leader does not have a can-do attitude, nobody will.

Consistent: A leader's attitude must remain relatively consistent so that others will know what to expect. It is hard to trust someone who has a constantly changing attitude.

Energetic: People absorb energy from energetic people—energizing others is a leader's duty.

Enthusiastic: People love interacting with enthusiastic people—enthusiasm is exciting and magnetic.

Inspiring: Inspiring others is one of a leader's most important responsibilities.

Go-getter: The leader must be gung-ho when something needs to get done. The leader must be ready to tackle the task at hand or nobody else will.

Happy: People like to be around other happy people—happiness is contagious.

Respectful: A respectful attitude begets respect from others while disrespect begets disrespect.

Optimistic: An optimistic attitude give's others positive hope—a pessimistic attitude reduces it.

Positive: A positive attitude is very contagious and appreciated by others—a negative attitude is also very contagious and damaging (re: the old "one bad apple" saying).

Steady: Followers look to the leader to determine their own response or reaction to an event. A leader cannot let emotions drive his or her actions or attitude.

Attitude may not be a direct view of character because of the countless external factors that impact it, but it does offer a good proxy view.

CHAPTER 13

Authenticity

Authenticity is how open, genuine, and transparent a person is with others. It is being truly the kind of person others believe we are—not counterfeit or fake. It is a person's genuineness, sincerity, realness, or legitimacy. Being authentic is being who we really are—transparent and genuine.

Authenticity is critical to leaders because it is directly correlated to a leader's legitimacy, honesty, and trustworthiness. A leader's true character and nature become obvious to others in time; even the best of actors cannot hide these for long. If a leader is found out to not be what others have been led to believe, he is doomed as dishonest and untrustworthy. The best course of action is to not even try to be someone or something we are not, even if who we really are is not the kind of person we need to be. If that is true, we should begin the process of changing ourselves into the kind of people we need to be. The discomfort with not being the kind of people we should be is great motivation to change and everyone has the ability to become any kind of person he or she wishes.

The following quotes support the value of authenticity:

The secret of success is sincerity.

—Jean Giraudoux, French novelist, essayist, and diplomat

Three things cannot be long hidden: the sun, the moon, and the truth.

—Buddha, spiritual teacher and founder of Buddhism

Our true self, character, and nature always come out—no worries if we are who we say we are.

CHAPTER 14

Behavior

Behavior is the way people act, how they conduct themselves, their actions, the activities they participate in, and their deeds and habits. Everyone has heard the old saying, "Actions speak louder than words." This saying simply means that people notice what you do more than they hear what you say. Leaders think of themselves as actors who are always on stage, always being watched and evaluated, because they are. Behaviors tell others an enormous amount of information about our true character.

Leaders of character demand behavioral standards above normal standards because of the leader's responsibility to set the example. A leader's every action is subject to scrutiny, and the more influence a leader has, the greater the scrutiny and exaggerated expectations.

> Nothing is so contagious as example; and we never do
> any great good or evil which does not produce its like.
> —Francois de La Rochefoucauld, French author of
> maxims on motive and self-interest

This powerful quote from de La Rochefoucauld illustrates how important it is that leaders never underestimate the power of their example because their most significant influence results from their behaviors, actions, and activities—their example. The importance of behavior is also championed by another frequently repeated popular leadership saying "lead by example" because people naturally mimic the example leaders set.

> Example is leadership.
> —Albert Schweitzer, theologian, philosopher,
> physician, and medical missionary

A leader of character is always out front, onstage, modeling the way; always setting the right example—always!

An important point about behavior that all leaders must be especially aware of is our natural inclination toward bias in judging our own behavior. It is self-protective human nature to judge ourselves by our intentions, not our actions, but judge others by their actions, regardless of their intentions. In many situations we will easily excuse ourselves, let ourselves off the hook, or create and accept excuses for our own poor or wrong behavior, while simultaneously disdaining others for the same behavior. This fault is often displayed by high profile or successful people in the news after they are caught doing something wrong, immoral, unethical, or illegal. Lance Armstrong famously stated that he did not consider seven years of doping for the Tour de France cheating; instead, he thought of it as leveling the field. Leaders must be vigilant to protect against this natural propensity and consciously be certain to judge ourselves by our behaviors and actions, not our intentions, no matter how good our intentions are.

> Hold yourself responsible for a higher standard than
> anyone else expects of you. Never excuse yourself.
> —Henry Ward Beecher, nineteen-century clergyman,
> social reformer, and abolitionist

Leaders are also very aware that a single bad or poorly thought-out action or behavior can have disastrous results, completely derailing everything a leader might have accomplished. When trust, respect, or integrity are destroyed by behavior unbecoming a leader, it can never be fully regained. People may forgive, but they never forget—years can be spent building trust, but it can be destroyed in a moment by poor behavior.

> It is in your moments of decision that your destiny is
> shaped.
> —Tony Robbins, self-help author and motivational
> speaker

A leader's influence is shaped significantly by behavior, because behavior is a public display of character.

CHAPTER 15

Charisma

Charisma is a combination of personality traits, behaviors, and people skills that other people are unusually drawn to. It is a person's magnetism, charm, and likableness. Webster's definition[8], "a personal magic of leadership arousing special popular loyalty or enthusiasm," goes even further in designating charisma as a leadership quality. The following quote points out that charisma is an intangible force causing visible effects (a definition very similar to leadership's).

> Charisma was originally a religious term, meaning "of the spirit" or "inspired." It's about letting God's light shine through us. Charisma is a sparkle in people that money can't buy. It's an invisible energy with visible effects.
> —Marianne Williamson, spiritual activist, author, and lecturer

---

[8] Merriam-Webster. http://www.merriam-webster.com/dictionary/charisma. Web. 19 June 2013

The following quote suggests that charisma is actually a leader's ability to convey or transmit enthusiasm, excitement, exuberance, or passion to others—an incredibly powerful skill.

> Charisma is the transference of enthusiasm.
> —Ralph Archbold, speaker, entertainer, performer

Having charisma means having the ability to infect others with your enthusiasm and passion.

The following quotes suggest that being a good leader of character is important in developing charisma.

> Charisma is the result of effective leadership, not the other way around.
> —Warren Bennis, pioneer of the contemporary field of leadership studies

> Charismatic leaders generally exhibit such attributes as extraordinary emotional expressiveness, self-confidence, self-determination, and freedom from internal conflict.
> —Jay Alden Conger and Rabindra Nath Kanungo, *Charismatic Leadership: The Elusive Factor in Organizational Effectiveness*

While it is easy to accept that charisma is valuable to leaders and their level of influence with followers, it does seem to be a rare trait, so we have to wonder if charismatic people are born with charisma. Certainly some people are naturally inclined towards personality traits that lead to charisma, but no one is born with it. Charisma is a learned and developed set of attributes or skills that comes through much practice and an intimate understanding of people: what moves them, what ignites them, what motivates them, etc. Even people who are more naturally inclined toward charisma must develop and refine their inclination just like any other talent, but everyone is capable of developing their own levels of charisma.

There is a dark side to charisma as well. Charisma has been scorned by some because too many highly charismatic people have used charisma for their own selfish advantage or to gain high profile or high impact leadership or management positions, only to ultimately fail because of their weak underlying character or substance. The misuse of charisma by unethical people with weak character has resulted in the term *charismatic* becoming somewhat of a derogatory description. However, leaders who remain very aware of this issue and are extremely careful to avoid it should not hesitate to take advantage of the power of charisma. It should be thought of like it is dynamite—very powerful and beneficial if used properly, but extremely dangerous if used improperly. Good, strong character in conjunction with charisma can undoubtedly result in spectacular leadership results, while bad character mixed with charisma can result in spectacular failure.

One of the main reasons charisma is so important to leaders is because a major key to charisma is spectacular communications abilities. Charismatic people have an ability to draw others in with their words, language, body language, and listening skills. They are expert at message delivery and the use of descriptive, vivid, image-based language and concepts that seem to paint a clear, verbal picture for others. Moreover, charismatic people are also adept, active listeners who make certain that the person they are listening to knows that what they are saying is important. Charismatic people make sure others know that what they say matters; therefore, a requirement of charisma is compassion and respect. The following quote illustrates this.

> How can you have charisma? Be more concerned
> about making others feel good about themselves than
> you are making them feel good about you.
> —Dan Reiland, executive pastor, author

Leaders of character listen—truly listen—with ears, mind, body, and eyes.

Charisma, like leadership, is a very young science that has not received as much focus as leadership, but we do know it is helpful in increasing our likability, and hence, our influence. The power of charisma on a leader's likeability has certainly been widely acknowledged. Following is a list of suggestions on how to develop character from Dale Carnegie's (1888-1955) *How to Win Friends and Influence People*,[9] still one of the most cited and impactful works on charisma and people skills available.

Become a friendlier person; increase your likability:

1. Don't criticize, condemn, or complain.
2. Give honest, sincere appreciation.

---

[9] Carnegie, Dale. *How to Win Friends and Influence People*. New York. Simon & Shuster. 1936, 1964, 1981. Print.

3. Arouse in the other person an eager want.

4. Become genuinely interested in other people.

5. Smile.

6. Remember that a person's name is to that person the sweetest and most important sound in any language.

7. Be a good listener.

8. Talk in terms of the other person's interests.

9. Make the other person feel important—do it sincerely.

Charisma is a leader's likability and influence magnifier.

CHAPTER 16

Commitment

Commitment is the act or pledge of holding oneself to being obligated and dedicated to an action, cause, duty, principles, position, vow, etc. It is our personal devotion and self-policed obligation to whatever the target is. Commitment is how mentally bound we are, emotionally and intellectually, to the cause or course of action.

Commitment is a strength-of-mind trait because it illustrates the sturdiness, tenacity, or vigor of a person's mental or cognitive control. Strength-of-mind traits are determined and controlled by the vitality or robustness of a part of our mind that is mostly beyond our conscious understanding. Similar to state-of-mind traits, we have some ability to consciously influence, control, or direct a strength-of-mind trait like commitment, but because so much of our strength of mind lies beyond our conscious understanding, conscious control or direction is limited. We simply cannot rely on our conscious mind to maintain a strength-of-mind trait over the long term because our conscious minds are always busy and fully dedicated to our everyday lives, responsibilities, problems, competing priorities, etc. Therefore, just as with state-of-mind traits, because so much of our strength-of-mind traits is beyond our conscious understanding, the best strategy for leaders is a continuous focus on character development. Becoming a person of stronger, more positive, and more virtuous character will result in a in a stronger, more positive, and more virtuous strength of mind as well.

This abstract discussion also points to an important synergistic cycle. Being a leader takes major commitment. Becoming a leader of character adds considerably to the amount of commitment required; consequently, the key to developing a greater ability to maintain commitment is to develop a stronger, more positive, and more virtuous character. Of course, developing that kind of character also requires a lot of commitment, which fully illustrates how synergistic and interrelated character and commitment are. A leader of character needs commitment and character equally, so they must be developed equally.

Most anyone with considerable life experience certainly knows that substantial commitment is required in every significant endeavor or accomplishment. Leaders know that the larger the impact we wish to have on the world, the more commitment is going to be required.

Nothing—*nothing!*—of great significance has ever been achieved without great commitment.

A leader's commitment is important because many (most?) people seem to be naturally prone to not being very committed and to giving up at the first sign of difficulty or failure. To offset this natural tendency and to set the right example, successful leaders go all-in fully expecting to accept difficulty and failures simply as lessons. In life, commitment is what sets the very successful apart from everyone else. One fantastic example is Thomas Edison. While attempting to invent the lightbulb, his first thousand attempts failed. When asked about how he could endure such failure, Edison replied, "We now know a thousand ways not to build a lightbulb." The world is lucky he was so committed.

> There's no abiding success without commitment.
> —Anthony Robbins, self-help author and
> motivational speaker

True commitment is revealed over time—sometimes a span of years. Anyone can be committed in the short term, but it takes genuine commitment to stay the course over years or decades. Mother Teresa and Gandhi committed their entire adult lives to their causes. The following incredibly powerful quote points out several important aspects of commitment, including its connection to character. Read it carefully and think about the meaning in each sentence to fully grasp the power in what it says.

> Commitment is what transforms a promise into
> reality. It is the words that speak boldly of your
> intentions. And the actions which speak louder than
> the words. It is making the time when there is none.
> Coming through time after time after time, year after
> year after year. Commitment is the stuff character is
> made of; the power to change the face of things. It is
> the daily triumph of integrity over skepticism.
> —Anonymous

It is obvious that commitment is critical to leaders for many reasons, but most importantly because if the leader is not committed, followers, nor anyone else will be either. Also, since the leader is guiding change in a specific direction, it takes commitment to stay the course through thick and thin or else the direction will become random and unfocused, which will cause followers to abandon ship for a clearer, smoother path. Plus, a leader's commitment is contagious; it gives followers the motivation they need to commit themselves, which is another important leadership duty.

Leaders are also vigilant to be aware of what deserves their commitment— and what does not. Many of the "fires" that have a way of consuming our time do not deserve any commitment, but we are all susceptible to getting bogged down in them. Some of the hardest leadership decisions require the leader to say "no" to things that do not deserve commitment. Sometimes, that's called growing up.

Without commitment to the right things, there is no progress; the more significant the advancement, the more commitment is required.

CHAPTER 17

Communication Skills

Communication skills are simply a person's ability to convey information to others through a variety of means such as speaking and writing, but also through less apparent means such as body language and other nonverbal actions. The importance of communication skills is repeated many times throughout this book because communicating is one of a leader's most vital duties. Much of a leader's influence—possibly most of it—comes through his or her ability to communicate well. What makes communications skills so important is people's need for clarity and simplicity. People benefit from clear and concise ideas, directions, expectations, and vision.

Communications is such an immense and important topic to people in all walks of life that there are entire college programs and degrees on the topic. Noting such enormity, it is safe to say that leaders can spend their lives developing and improving their communications skills. The subject is much too huge to cover in this book, but a few aspects that are essential to leaders can be pointed out. These include:

- **Casual conversation/small talk:** Striking up and carrying on a conversation with strangers is a feat that few do well, and because of that rarity, the value of the skill is enormous. Some keys to casual conversation include having some knowledge of the person you are talking to or something in common with them, having something to talk about by staying up to date on news and current events, and keeping in mind that the best topic of conversation is the person you are talking to.

- **Public speaking:** People say they fear public speaking more than death, which means being a good public speaker is important to every leader because followers will always expect the leader to stand up and speak so they do not have to. Preparation and practice are key to becoming a good public speaker. Courage and audacity are also helpful.

- **Presentations:** Presentations are along the same lines as public speaking but include the requirement to be adept with audiovisual/multimedia programs and technology.

- **Word choice:** The words a leader uses in his or her communications are critical because words not only define the message, they also say a lot about the speaker. Leaders are conscious to choose their words carefully in order to fit the audience and the circumstances.

- **Writing:** Because of our modern high-tech, high-speed world of texting and instant messaging, proper and correct writing and grammar are more important than ever. The skill of writing clearly and professionally is critical because meaning and intent must be easily distinguishable.

- **Listening:** It may seem odd that listening is mentioned several times in this book as an aspect of communications, but for a leader it may be one of the more important facets. Because leadership is about relationships, listening is key in developing and maintaining any relationship. Most people spend their listening time preparing a response to what is being said, but great listening means giving our complete attention to the speaker and listening with our ears, eyes, body language, and mind.

One of the most sincere forms of respect is actually listening to what another has to say.
—Bryant H. McGill, American editor and author

- **Body language:** Seventy percent or more of what we communicate is nonverbal signals and body language. This mode of communicating includes things like eye contact, facial expressions, gestures, posture, stance, tone of voice, and even barely perceptible actions like a brief nod of the head, raising of an eyebrow, shrug of the shoulder, or widening/narrowing of the eyes. Studying, learning, and using body language and nonverbal communications is very beneficial for leaders.

The human body is the best picture of the human soul.
—Ludwig Wittgenstein, Austrian/British philosopher

- **Emotional awareness:** Emotional awareness is being knowledgeable and cognizant of your own and other people's emotions. Emotions are extraordinarily powerful and can cause people to be unpredictable and do things they normally would not. Leaders are aware of the power of emotions and work to understand and control them.

The best way to develop or improve all of these aspects of communication skills is through intentional practice. Leaders seek out opportunities to write, speak, and socialize. Taking speaking and writing classes is advantageous if possible, as is listening to great speeches and reading great books. There is no shortage of resources or opportunities to improve our communications skills.

A leader's most important duty is communicating—the better she is at it, the better a leader she is.

Following are a few suggestions to help develop communication skills:

- Take public speaking classes.
- Read. Reading involves us with words, sentence structure, grammar, etc.
- Listen to books. Same as reading books, but with the added element of hearing it.
- Watch other speakers. Closely watching great speakers on video or DVD will give us examples and hints we can incorporate into our own speaking.
- Teach. Teaching forces you to speak in front of groups.
- Practice speaking, even in private. Film yourself so you can see where you might improve.

CHAPTER 18

Compassion

Compassion is a heartfelt and genuine concern for others. It is a feeling of sympathy and desire to help or aid others, especially in times of distress, suffering, or misfortune. In terms of leadership, compassion is simply a genuine concern for others. Compassion must unquestionably be a hallmark of leaders of character; leaders who want to make a positive impact on the world inherently care deeply about others.

Leaders understand that leadership is serving others, putting other's needs ahead of our own, and even putting other people's needs ahead of our own rights sometimes. To do this, to serve others, leaders must genuinely care about them; it is impossible to serve people we do not care about.

An important parallel concept to compassion is *kindness*. Kindness means being friendly, caring, considerate, courteous, and generous—all traits that must be synonymous with every leader of character. We all have someone in our life or in our past whom we would consider the kindest person we ever knew, and we all know how much influence that person has or had on us. Hence, the influence kindness creates is why kindness is important to leaders. As leaders, sometimes we have to put duty or the benefit of all ahead of kindness, but we all know how vital being kind is to our leadership influence.

> No act of kindness, however small, is ever wasted.
> —Aesop (620-564 BC), ancient Greek fabulist and storyteller

> Constant kindness can accomplish much. As the sun makes ice melt, kindness causes misunderstanding, mistrust and hostility to evaporate.
> —Albert Schweitzer, theologian, philosopher, physician, and medical missionary

A leader's kindness is repaid with respect and amplified influence.

One note of caution must be established here: leaders must be aware that too much compassion or kindness is detrimental, or even destructive. Too much compassion, kindness, generosity, or sympathy will result in us overextending ourselves or our resources, which could result in us, or the people we are responsible for, suffering. For instance, if we gave away all of our money (and there is no end to the charitable need for money), then we would in fact be condemning ourselves and our families when we are not be able to pay our own bills. So while we must care about others, our compassion and kindness has to be consciously measured in order to not endanger our own welfare or ability to lead.

Still another issue for leaders to be aware of is occasionally our responsibility or duty must supersede compassion. This passage from General Colin Powell illustrates the point perfectly:

> Good leadership involves responsibility to the welfare of the group, which means that some people will get angry at your actions and decisions. It's inevitable if you're honorable. Trying to get everyone to like you is a sign of mediocrity: You'll avoid the tough decisions, you'll avoid confronting the people who need to be confronted, and you'll avoid offering differential rewards based on differential performance because some people might get upset. Ironically, by procrastinating on the difficult choices, by trying not to get anyone mad, and by treating everyone equally "nicely" regardless of their contributions, you'll simply ensure that the only people you'll wind up angering are the most creative and productive people in the organization.
> —General Colin Powell, American statesman and retired four-star Army general

Leaders of character are conscious of the need for compassion, and the need to maintain control of it.

A leader does not exist without compassion for others, but a leader with too much ceases to be a leader.

CHAPTER 19

Competence

Competence is the designation given a person of advanced ability, skill, or expertise in a given field or activity. Rather than indicating some varying measure or level of ability, being competent is having reached the level of being well qualified and able to demonstrate adequate ability or proficiency. Competence is almost an all-or-nothing trait.

Leaders must be competent in at least two major areas: leadership expertise and technical expertise. This book addresses leadership expertise, whereas technical expertise refers to the technical aspects of the leader's specific situation, organization, or whatever it is being led. For example, a leader in the classroom must be competent in how to run a classroom, and a leader in a manufacturing operation must be competent in manufacturing. A leader will absolutely fail, regardless of leadership expertise, if he or she does not know or understand what is going on. In fact, the importance of competence can best be illustrated by its opposite: incompetence. Incompetence needs no explanation; everyone knows an incompetent leader will not be a leader for long.

> A competent leader can get efficient service from poor troops, while on the contrary, an incapable leader can demoralize the best of troops.
> —John J. Pershing, World War I general

Level of competence is directly related to a leader's level of influence.

Intuition and instinct, often cited as key leadership skills, are intricately related to competence. Intuition and instinct (an inner voice) are difficult (or impossible) to manage or manipulate, but they develop naturally in conjunction with competence, experience, knowledge, and wisdom. The more competent we become, the more we develop instinct and intuition. The more experience we have; the more we rely on gut feelings.

Most important to leaders is that we have complete control over our own competence; it is not based on nature, chance, or genetics. Our level of competence is completely our choice; it is determined by the amount of effort we put into developing it through learning and experience. Given the rapidly changing and advancing world, it is a guarantee that we will never be too competent; it is something we will work on for life. In fact, if we don't work on our competence continuously, the world will simply pass us by and leave us behind.

Competence is readily accessible to any leader willing to earn it—anyone not willing will be left behind.

CHAPTER 20

Confidence

Confidence is a feeling of self-assurance, brass, certitude, or conviction. In this context confidence can be thought of as self-confidence: certainty, confidence and self-assurance in our own abilities, competence, knowledge, judgment, etc. Other aspects of confidence include

- **Exhibited Self-Confidence:** the self-confidence and self-assurance that others see that we possess
- **Confidence Others Place in Us:** others' belief and trust in us and our abilities, competence, judgment, etc.
- **Confidence We Place in Others:** the confidence and trust we place in others' abilities, competence, judgment, etc.

For leaders, self-confidence is the most critical because the others are built upon it—it has to be developed first for the other three to exist. General George Patton said, "Self-confidence and leadership are twin brothers." His legendary self-confidence was one of the most effective tools he used to motivate his soldiers. The self-confidence that Patton exhibited told the soldiers he was extremely confident in himself, and that built their self-confidence.

A leader's confidence is as important to followers as it is to the leader because it is so contagious—lack of confidence is just as contagious.

Confidence, especially self-confidence, is another strength-of-mind trait. Much of what creates self-confidence is beyond our understanding, but again, our best strategy in developing confidence is in developing our character. The following quote connects confidence to character and the elements.

> Confidence … thrives on honesty, on honor, on the sacredness of obligations, on faithful protection and on unselfish performance. Without them it cannot live.
> —Franklin D. Roosevelt, thirty-second president of the United States

Confidence grows as our character strengthens.

One of a leader's duties is to help others develop their own self-confidence. One way leaders do that is by placing their confidence in them. It is motivational when a leader shows confidence in a follower; it motivates that person to rise to a challenge and accomplish more than he or she otherwise would have. There are countless stories of people overcoming the odds because of confidence gained from others.

Leaders must be wary of how self-confidence is interpreted to avoid over-confidence appearing as arrogance. Arrogance is extremely detrimental to a leader because no one likes it and few will tolerate it. Confidence

and arrogance are completely different attributes, but the d
when over-confidence gives the appearance of arrogance.

A leader's confidence is interrelated and proportional to most of the
elements, especially competence, credibility, and knowledge. In a
somewhat virtuous cycle, the more we know about a subject, or the
better we are at a task, the more confident we are; the more confident we
are, the better we get at what we do. A great example is public speaking.
Great speakers get great by doing it, a lot—practicing for countless hours
and making lots of speeches. Impressive and very confident speakers or
statesmen usually have years of experience and practice behind their
confidence.

Other significant correlations include authenticity, honesty, honor,
integrity, morality, trustworthiness, and values. A rise or decrease in
any of them will result in the same change in our self-confidence; in
fact, this points to one very important value of our moral character. Self-
confidence is bolstered when we are ethical, genuine, honest, honorable,
and moral because of the decrease in worry and stress from not having to
remember or cover up poor or unethical behavior. A similar correlation
could be traced between self-confidence and most of the other elements,
thereby supporting the validity of the suggestion to develop confidence
by developing character.

**Confidence is a part of every leader beginning with the
self-confidence to step up and lead.**

CHAPTER 21

Courage

Courage is the ability to face and withstand fear. It is bravery in the face of danger or peril, real or perceived. It is our personal ability to face or do what we are afraid to face or do. Courage is backbone, boldness, daring, guts, mettle, and nerve—all extremely essential qualities and behaviors for leaders. Much of the value of leadership comes from the fact that simply stepping up to lead requires such significant courage—and such courage is rare.

> Courage is being scared to death, but saddling up anyway.
> —John Wayne, film actor, director, and producer

> Courage is doing what you are afraid to do.
> —Eddie Rickenbacker, American World War I ace pilot

> You will never do anything in this world without courage. It is the greatest quality of the mind next to honor.
> —Aristotle (384-322 BC) classical Greek philosopher

Courage: the most important of all the virtues
because without courage, you can't practice any other
virtue consistently.
—Maya Angelou, American author and poet

Like John Wayne said, courage is simply the ability to face fear or do something in spite of being scared to death. It is not the absence of fear or fearlessness—that is not courage at all. In fact, fearlessness in a situation that should elicit fear is dangerous (or stupid). Fear is an innate safety mechanism meant to keep us from injury—without fear, the human race would not have lasted long. Even in social settings when physical harm is not a possibility, fear protects us emotionally to avoid humiliation, rejection, or failure. Fear makes us examine the situation more carefully in an attempt to avoid harm before we commit ourselves. Fear makes us smarter.

A synonym of courage—audacity—is itself an incredibly powerful leadership and success tool—that is, the audacity to decide that we are the ones who should step up to lead when leadership is needed. Audacity is the primary key to being a successful salesperson, because salespeople with the audacity to ask for the sale get the most sales, just as leaders with the most audacity to step up and lead are the most successful leaders. The extraordinary power and influence gained from having the audacity to be the one to step up and lead is something all leaders of character should strive for.

The first quality that is needed is audacity.
—Winston Churchill, prime minister of England and
statesman

> Success is the child of audacity.
> —Benjamin Disraeli, British prime minister,
> parliamentarian, statesman

Audacity may be a leader's most powerful talent, skill, tool, and gift.

In today's high productivity working world, it has become an accepted reality that if we are not messing up sometimes, not making mistakes, or failing occasionally, we are just not doing enough; we are not pushing the envelope far enough. Courage is required to pursue a path that could very well be the wrong path. What's more, in our quickly advancing world, leaders will be increasingly faced with decisions or choosing a direction without having nearly enough information to make a completely educated decision. Incredible courage is required to head off into such unknown and uncharted territory as our world is becoming.

> Sometimes, when you're the leader, you have to jump
> off the cliff then build your wings and learn how to
> fly on the way down.
> —Phillip Rozeman, MD-cardiologist and community
> leader

To lead means we have to risk failing, finding out we're incompetent, or being proven wrong. That is a tall order for our fragile human psyches to accept, but that is also why there is such a vital need for courageous leaders of character.

Simply stepping up to lead and putting yourself out there takes uncommon courage—therein is one reason leaders are so important.

CHAPTER 22

Creativity

Creativity is the mental ability to generate new or innovative solutions, ideas, or alternatives that may be useful in solving a problem or in communicating with others. Leadership creativity includes the ability to create a mental picture of a goal or desirable future or destination, communicate that vision to followers, and then creatively figure out how to make it a reality.

Creativity is important for leaders because change is inherent in leadership. Leaders must have the creativity and ability to develop the idea of what the change or impact should look like or where it should lead, and then create the process to make it become a reality. Today's high-tech, fast-paced, ever-changing world is only making creativity, imagination, and innovation even more valuable and vital.

> Creativity requires the courage to let go of certainties.
> —Erich Fromm, German social psychologist and
> philosopher

Any discussion of creativity brings up the question, Are creative people born creative, or is it a developable skill? The answer is probably some of both, but regardless, it can be developed, at least to a point, whether we are naturally creative or not. Michelangelo, one of the greatest artists of all time, and obviously very creative, said, "If people knew how hard I worked to get my mastery, it wouldn't seem so wonderful at all." This statement means that even if he were naturally creative and talented, he still had to work hard to develop it. So while some people may be naturally more creative than others, creativity is definitely a learnable and developable skill.

Leadership is about change; creativity is required to drive change in the right direction.

CHAPTER 23

Credibility

Credibility is the level of belief, confidence, and trust that others have in a person's honesty, competence, trustworthiness, or abilities. It is the measure of a person's believability or capability and the level of faith and confidence that followers have in a leader's reliability and expertise. Credibility is about a leader's overall trustworthiness as a leader.

A leader's credibility = competence + trustworthiness + reliability.

A leader's credibility is important in all relevant areas, but especially in technical expertise and leadership proficiency. Technical credibility comes from being very good at the trade, skill, or whatever the leadership situation involves. For example, if leading in a construction situation, technical credibility comes from being very good at construction. Nobody will influence any situation without technical credibility because followers must believe the leader knows what he or she is doing. Leadership credibility comes from being very good at leadership. Leader of character credibility comes from being good at character-based leadership and all of the elements of leaders of character. No one will be influenced unless they have faith in the leader's leadership ability.

Credibility is not a quantifiable or measureable element; it is pretty much all or nothing: we either have credibility, or we don't. Additionally, because credibility is in the eyes of the beholder; a leader may never really know how much credibility he or she has with followers because there is little way to gauge it. While great credibility may never be acknowledged, it is certainly obvious to everyone when someone loses their credibility. News like that travels fast and far.

Credibility is also directly correlated with several of the other elements, especially authenticity, behavior, commitment, communication skills, competence, honesty, honor, integrity, knowledge, morals, professionalism, respect, responsibility, and trustworthiness. A rise or drop in any of them will cause the corresponding movement in credibility. Credibility's direct connection to trust means that, like trust, once we have credibility, if we sacrifice it, it will never be regained to the same level again. Therefore, leaders must ferociously protect their own credibility.

All of the correlations to the other elements also point to credibility's most important correlation: its direct relationship with influence. To have any influence, a leader must be a credible person.

A leader's level of credibility is directly proportional to his level of influence.

CHAPTER 24

Discipline

Discipline is the self-commitment and self-regulation of managing and controlling one's own actions and behaviors. *Discipline* and *self-discipline* are used interchangeably in this context because the subject here is an individual, a leader. Discipline is keeping our nose to the grindstone—our self-command, self-control, self-guidance, self-regulation, and self-restraint. Discipline is a leader's ability to focus and persist specifically on relevant tasks and in continuing through mundane or difficult activities or processes to completion.

Discipline is the critical ingredient in all self-mastery; it is the ultimate aspiration of leaders of character.

Discipline is another of the strength-of-mind traits that is determined and controlled by the tenacity or vigor of a subconscious part of our mind that is mostly beyond our conscious control. We do have some conscious influence and control of our discipline, but again, since most of our strength of mind is beyond our conscious understanding, the most significant impact we can have is through our own character development, which also develops our strength of mind.

Discipline is vital to leaders because we are naturally prone to distraction and changing interests, especially when the going gets tough. Sometimes, to stay on track, we need all of the self-discipline we can muster to force ourselves to buckle down and be responsible. In fact, discipline is most required when we are least motivated. Additionally, most major achievements in life are the result of some long-term process. Major self-discipline is always required to stay the course through any extended major process. Becoming a great a leader, especially a great leader of character, is just such a process. It is practically a lifelong process, requiring possibly the most discipline of any process in our lifetime.

Any significant end will always require significant discipline.

Following are some powerful quotes that illustrate the importance of discipline:

> Discipline is the refining fire by which talent becomes ability.
> —Roy L. Smith, Christian author

The previous quote means natural talent is useless without the discipline required to turn it into real skill or ability. Actually, natural-born talent is completely wasted without the discipline that is absolutely required to develop it into something beneficial.

> Discipline is the bridge between goals and accomplishment.
> —Jim Rohn, American entrepreneur, author, and motivational speaker

If I want to be great, I have to win the victory over
myself … self-discipline.
—Harry S. Truman, thirty-third president of the
United States

Greatness at anything requires magnificent greatness at self-discipline.

With self-discipline most anything is possible.
—Theodore Roosevelt, twenty-sixth president of the
United States

One important need for discipline rests with another of our natural
tendencies to always be on the lookout for a short-cut or the easiest
path. It seems to be human nature to naturally choose the easier path
to a lesser achievement rather than a more difficult path to a greater
achievement. In other words, many people, maybe most, readily accept
a lower level of success because it is easier to achieve. This natural
propensity may also illustrate the rarity of discipline as well as many of
the other elements in this book.

Discipline is certainly required in planning ahead and in preparations
to carry plans out—both very important duties of leaders. Leaders must
be proactive by thinking and working ahead or considering potential
problems. Without the discipline to plan ahead, we are inclined to be
reactive, or just doing what has to be done to get by—and nothing great
ever came from that.

Similarly, discipline is one weapon in our battle against one of our most powerful enemies: procrastination. Most of us are victims of procrastination—there is probably not a human being on the planet who does not fight the monster. There never seems to be enough hours in the day to get everything done anyway, so it is very easy to fall into the habit of always working under the stress of deadlines. College students are especially notorious for procrastination. They habitually wait until the last minute to study for exams or work on assignments, even though the habit results in a massive increase in stress and does little in increasing knowledge.

Discipline is not a trait or skill like riding a bicycle that we can develop and never lose; it demands constant attention. Yesterday's discipline no longer exists and today's discipline must be developed today. As previously mentioned, the best way to develop discipline is through character development, but we also have to give it serious conscious effort as well.

Discipline is a leader's weapon in the battle against human tendencies to take short-cuts, choose the easy way out, procrastinate, and lose focus.

CHAPTER 25

Flexibility/Adaptability

Flexibility is a person's inclination toward accepting and molding with change. **Adaptability** is the inclination to be malleable and self-adjusting to fit in. Implicit in flexibility and adaptability is an acceptance of, and even proclivity for, change.

Leadership is using influence to cause intentional change, so leaders must certainly be flexible and adaptable. Growth, progress, advancement, improvement, expansion, development, or innovation do not take place without change, and if nothing is changing or happening, there's nothing to lead. In fact, when someone steps up to become a leader, he or she also accepts the task of being a *change agent*. Change agents are people who proactively cause change, transformation, growth, expansion, or improvement with an intended result in mind.

Leaders must always beware of the unbelievably difficult part of being a change agent: the vicious resistance to change that most people are prone to. This frustrating and brutal part of being a change agent is well documented and written about often. Generally speaking, the longer people have been doing something, the harder they will fight change. It is human nature to become comfortable and complacent over time, remaining in the same position, which naturally makes us very protective of that position and the way we've always done it.

The problem for change agents is this complacency and protectionism can, and does, stand in the way of progress. Change is one of only a few things that are guaranteed, and the change that is going to happen will either be progress or decline. Change agents are responsible for making change be progress. Most importantly, there really is no such thing as status quo or stasis; everyone, everything, and every organization is either progressing or declining at all times. So if a person, group, or organization appears to be stationary or static, they are actually declining and the progressing world is passing them by.

With resistance to change a reality in any leadership situation, leaders accept the responsibility that they must sometimes make people angry in order to make positive change happen. General Colin Powell supported the premise when he said that being a responsible leader means ticking people off sometimes. Change agents must always keep the welfare of the many ahead of the feelings of the few, regardless of who the few are.

In order to combat long-term tenure complacency, some organizations even institute processes that force change. One example is the United States military. Military officers hold positions or commands for a few years at most before they are required to move to another position or leave the military. This process not only reduces complacency, it also creates continuous opportunity for advancement for junior personnel. In fact, take out opportunity for advancement and the only people who will be left are those with little ambition or initiative—not a recipe for success in today's world.

Probably the main benefit is that the change in jobs forces people to learn new skills and processes, which is itself energizing and rejuvenating, and it makes them more valuable to the organization. The downside of such a system is the potential loss of valuable people in their positions; however, the overall benefits for the entire organization outweigh the individual losses.

Forced change also ensures a stream of fresh ideas, new ways of looking at things, youthful energy, and rejuvenated interest into all the different levels of the organization. There is little that is sadder or more detrimental than a leader who overstays his or her effectiveness or efficiency. For leaders in competitive market organizations, this scenario is truly complicated because of the traditional high value placed on longevity (seniority) and perceived loyalty illustrated by long-term tenure. It is not easy to fault someone who may have given decades or his or her entire adult life to an organization. Complicating the issue further is the damage is usually not obvious or visible because it is damage through missed growth, opportunities, or advancement.

Change! Cause it! Since it's going to happen anyway, make it what it should be.

This situation, and the answer to it, is much too complex to be resolved here; however, leaders must be aware of it and be prepared to face it. Leaders are responsible for finding ways to retain the wisdom and tacit knowledge of long-term people while also continuously developing their replacements. Leaders should always be developing and grooming replacements—even for themselves. Actually, one sign of great leaders is they openly develop their own replacements.

Leaders must also remain aware of their own need to change and grow. Just as muscles atrophy without use, so too does everything about us, mentally and physically. Therefore, we should always be growing mentally, spiritually, experientially, emotionally, and personally by continuing to learn, seeking new experiences, and remaining physically active.

Leaders have no choice but to be flexible and adaptable because change and growth are an automatic part of every leader's life.

CHAPTER 26

Honesty

Honesty is being just, sticking to the facts and truth, and having no intention of deception or devious motives in any way. It is a measure of truthfulness, straightforwardness, fairness, sincerity, and uprightness. Being honest is refusing to deceive or gain unfair advantage, especially by fraudulent means.

Honesty is being honorable in behavior and intentions.

Following are some quotes that illustrate what honesty is and the value of it:

> He that loseth his honesty hath nothing else to lose.
> —John Lyly, English writer, poet, dramatist,
> and politician

> Honesty is something you can't wear out.
> —Waylon Jennings, country music singer,
> songwriter, and musician

Honesty is the first chapter in the book of wisdom.
—Thomas Jefferson, American founding father,
author of the Declaration of Independence, and third
president of the United States

A major issue with honesty must be openly addressed here for the benefit of every imperfect person reading this book. Honesty is demanded by all civilized societies, religious faiths, laws, honor codes, codes of ethics, etc. All the honesty quotes in this section raise honesty to one of the highest order standards of life itself, and we know that it is critical in maintaining every relationship in our lives, especially with our closest relationships. It is vital as well in maintaining our authenticity, credibility, honor, integrity, morality, respect, trustworthiness, and a strong, positive, and virtuous character.

All through life we are inundated with sayings like "honesty is the best policy," and "the truth will set you free," and George Washington's "I cannot tell a lie" sayings and proverbs. However, in spite of all of this pressure and focus, nobody is 100 percent honest, and probably nobody in the history of the planet was. Everyone breaks laws, lies, steals, and deceives. For example, how many of us break the speed limit or roll through an occasional stop sign without coming to a complete stop? That is breaking the law. How many of us have taken something home from work or school, even something as simple as a pencil or some paper? That is stealing. How many of us have withheld our honest opinion from someone because we didn't want them mad? That is lying and deceiving. And, how many of us are completely honest with children, especially when they are young and full of innocence and magic?

It's pointless to keep listing examples. If anyone has not done any of these or other actions along those lines, well, they are either superhuman or pathologically dishonest, even with themselves. It is likely that everyone could list several personal examples of instances in our own lives where we were and are not completely honest. The point is not to insult anyone or make anybody feel bad, but instead to point out that we are all imperfect and fallible. The point is to bring our attention to this human fact in order to compel us as leaders to become conscious of working on and controlling our fallibility.

So the question becomes, since we cannot be perfectly honest, where do we draw the line? Actually, we do not draw a line because that would create a static point just like the 100-percent-honest line that we cannot reach. Instead, we set and vehemently live by a standard based on honor, honorable living, and valuing our moral character as one of our highest priorities. Our honesty standard should be to always maintain our honor and moral character even if we cannot maintain complete honesty. We can be completely honorable because honor takes into account many factors that minimize our fallibility.

A warning though: care must be taken to never let ourselves weasel on this; we can never excuse or accept that any dishonesty is okay. Any dishonest action should cause shame because excusing or accepting any dishonesty would simply be lowering the standards to let ourselves off the hook, and that will always lead to lowering the standards again and again. Minor dishonesty for honorable reasons and intentions allows us a small, momentary pardon of our fallibility. As long as we keep any dishonesty under tight control and are never dishonest for nefarious, deceitful, or evil reasons we can be imperfectly honest and honorable as well.

There are also two components of honesty: honesty with ourselves and honesty with others. Being honest with ourselves means being brutally truthful in our self-view, especially about negative aspects and weaknesses that we would rather ignore (and usually do). Yes, brutal honesty with ourselves is absolutely the best way to live honorably, and perhaps the best self-management and self-mastery strategy available. Being brutally honest with ourselves is the only way to truly understand our strengths and weaknesses. Brutal honesty with ourselves is also the best way to help make the right choices and decisions. So much pain, failure, bad situations, and even financial ruin could be avoided if people could be more honest with themselves when making some choices and decisions, especially life-altering decisions.

Being honest with others is always being fair, just, and straight with honorable intentions. For leaders, there is an added facet of being honest without being hurtful; brutal honesty is unacceptable with others. Leaders must be honest with people while also working to maintain relationships while building people up. Brutal honesty can hurt relationships and it tears people down. Leaders simply cannot be as brutally honest with others as we can and should be with ourselves.

Dishonesty also has a way of taking on a life of its own and propagating more dishonesty. We all know the old saying that one lie leads to another, and another, and so on. Most of us experienced it firsthand as little kids when asked if we were responsible for something that we knew we were going to get in trouble for. Mothers are generally experts at proving the one-lie-leads-to-another point, and then we generally got in more trouble for lying about it than we would have if we had just admitted guilt to start with (at least for those of us who were always guilty). We often see the exact same scenario regularly played out by adults in politics as well. Dishonesty out of deceit or dishonorable intentions is always found out.

> A lie cannot live.
> —Martin Luther King Jr., clergyman and civil rights leader

One of the most important facets of honesty for leaders of character is its direct correlation to other principles such as authenticity, compassion, credibility, honor, morality/ethics, respect, and trustworthiness. All of these elements are connected and proportional to one another so damaging any one of them negatively impacts the others. A leader simply cannot be dishonest and maintain authenticity, compassion, credibility, honor, morality/ethics, respect, and trustworthiness.

Moreover, dishonesty in any of the roles we play in our life (father, mother, coworker, student, etc.) will impact all of our roles. Dishonesty at work or school will certainly have a negative impact at home, or vice-versa, because our subconscious and conscience dwell only on the dishonesty, regardless of the role. Therefore, the weight of dishonesty on our conscience will have a negative impact on our confidence and ability to perform in all aspects of our daily lives. A guilty conscience is something that is hard to get away from.

This powerful quote sums up the critical importance of honesty.

> Honesty is the cornerstone of all success, without which confidence and ability to perform shall cease to exist.
> —Mary Kay Ash, founder of Mary Kay Cosmetics

Wow, "shall cease to exist"—it just cannot get much more significant than that!

Success as a leader and in life is dependent upon honesty. Without it, the mandatory trust and support from others and the confidence and ability to perform at a level that will lead to success will not exist.

CHAPTER 27

Honor

Honor is a person's internal dedication to, and full acknowledgment of the value of an unshakable commitment to duty, compassion, credibility, fairness, honesty, humility, integrity, justice, responsibility, moral and ethical behavior, respect, responsibility, trustworthiness, and personal values. Honor is not abiding by any one or two of these; honor is a strong personal obligation to them all. Being honorable is strictly living with a sincere sense of honest, moral, and ethical conduct. For leaders, honor is the measure of how deeply and stalwartly we value, live every day by, protect, and hold ourselves to our duties, responsibilities, values, morality, integrity, and character.

The leader who cherishes his own honor will have little trouble with all of the other elements of leaders of character.

Our honor is gauged by how well the world sees us hold ourselves and others around us to doing right, and it is illustrated in our public defense and promotion of right, honesty, justice, responsibility, and duty. While it might seem old-fashioned in today's world, leaders of character understand the importance of behavior that is considered noble, valiant, respectful, chivalrous, and gallant. While these words are not used much today, there is absolutely nothing negative or detrimental about such behavior, and there is no doubt that the world would be better if the words and behavior were more prevalent.

Honor is the projection of the civility, decency, and nobility of our character and soul.

These quotes from people who had significant impacts on the world illustrate the elevated value of honor.

> I love the name of honor, more than I fear death.
> —Julius Caesar, Roman general and statesman

Death before dishonor.

> Who sows virtue reaps honor.
> —Leonardo da Vinci, Italian Renaissance painter, sculptor, architect, scientist, engineer, inventor

> All the great things are simple, and many can be expressed in a single word: freedom, justice, honor, duty, mercy, hope.
> —Winston Churchill, prime minister of England and statesman

Give up money, give up fame, give up science, give
the earth itself and all it contains, rather than do an
immoral act. And never suppose, that in any possible
situation, or under any circumstances, it is best for
you to do a dishonorable thing, however slightly so it
may appear to you. Whenever you are to do a thing,
though it can never be known but to yourself, ask
yourself how you would act were all the world looking
at you, and act accordingly.
—Thomas Jefferson, American founding father,
author of the Declaration of Independence, and third
president of the United States

Honor is one of the more difficult elements to define or describe
for several reasons. First of all, the word *honor* has multiple uses and
dictionary definitions besides how it is defined in this context. And
secondly, honor is such a lofty, abstract, and internal principle residing
deep within us—in our heart, mind, and moral character—which
makes the concept of honor extremely difficult to consciously grasp.
The definition, "the projection of the civility, decency, and nobility of
our character and soul," is indicative of just how lofty and intangible
honor is.

One place we can turn to in order to develop a clearer understanding of
honor is the United States military. Much like they have with leadership,
the US military has long understood and promoted the value of honor
and its associated behaviors. Honorable behavior is taught, promoted,
reinforced, and rewarded at all levels of the military; it is a major
component of the military culture and psyche. The culture of honor
that has been created in all branches ensures the military is rich in

honorable people at all levels because people with a high sense of honor are naturally drawn to the military in a virtuous cycle.

Civilian society would seriously benefit from a fraction of the prevalence and reverence of honor that is inherent in the military. Civilian leaders of character shoulder the mighty responsibility to promote, demonstrate, and reward honorable behavior in order to raise the principle's profile and value. Civilian organizations and communities would be drastically transformed with an increase in honor and honorable behavior—and such thinking and behavior begins with the leader.

> Honor is a matter of carrying out, acting, and living
> the values of respect, duty, loyalty, selfless service,
> integrity and personal courage in everything you do.
> —United States Army Core Values

> Honor ... Conduct ourselves in the highest ethical
> manner in all relationships ... Be honest and truthful
> in our dealings ... Abide by an uncompromising code
> of integrity, taking responsibility for our actions and
> keeping our word; Fulfill or exceed our legal and
> ethical responsibilities ... twenty-four hours a day.
> —United States Navy Core Values (abridged)

These statements give a clear understanding of what honor and honorable behavior is in the military. It is clear that honor is held in the highest esteem, as it should be in all walks of life. These passages, especially taken in context, are incredibly meaningful when we consider how many have given their own lives in support of duty, honor, and country.

> Duty, Honor, Country. Those three hallowed words
> reverently dictate what you ought to be, what you can
> be, what you will be.
> —Douglas MacArthur, general of the Army

Having an honor code and stringently living by it is an essential responsibility for leaders, just as it is for military personnel. Following is the honor code for the United States Air Force Academy: "We will not lie, steal, or cheat nor tolerate among us anyone who does."

The honor code for the US Military Academy at West Point: "A cadet will not lie, cheat, steal or tolerate those who do."

The honor code for the US Naval Academy: "A midshipman will not lie, cheat, or steal."

Navy's honor code does not have a "tolerate" clause like the USAFA and USMA because they believe that maintaining our own honor is our individual duty and policing honor should not be pressed upon others who might define honor differently or interpret a situation erroneously. Regardless, the standards and expectations are the same for all three academies because there is a lengthy, detailed honor concept and oath behind each of the honor codes that closes most any loophole a cadet or midshipman may find.

The few specific dishonorable actions specified in the codes—lying, cheating, stealing, and tolerating—seem to represent a bare minimum of expectations and standards, but in reality they truly define an overarching and all-encompassing set of expectations and behaviors. If we absolutely do not lie, cheat, steal, or tolerate anyone who does in every role we play, then there is no possibility that we would act out any other dishonorable, dishonest, immoral, or unethical behavior that is not listed. Holding ourselves to those four honorable behaviors naturally compels us to include all behaviors. Extrapolating all that the codes entail into everyday life helps ensure honorable behavior in everything we do. Borrowing from the academy codes, following is an easily adoptable code for leaders of characters:

A leader of character will not lie, cheat, steal, or tolerate anyone who does—to do so is choosing dishonor.

A more detailed and exacting honor code would be

> Leader of Character Honor Code: A leader of
> character is ethical, honest, moral, respectful, and
> trustworthy at all times; insists that others are as
> well; and rejects anyone who is not, because dishonor
> results from any of these.

One of the most important facets of honor is its significant connection to moral character. Honor is one of the major determinates of the thoughts, actions, and principles that ultimately decide and illustrate our moral character, which makes honor a major projection or surrogate of moral character. Therefore, to get some idea of our moral character, we can survey our honor. Leaders reap the benefit somewhere along the way because those who are fully committed to living with honor, and reinforce that commitment often, will be more likely to maintain honor and moral character when placed in a challenging situation—and we will all face challenging situations. Because honor is such a deep spiritual-like element connected to our humanity, honorable behavior results in palpable good feelings, pride, and contentment whereas dishonorable behavior always results in regret, shame, and discontentment. There is something within our humanity that promotes honor, and it is a leader's duty to support that natural goodness.

Living with honor—being authentic, compassionate, disciplined, ethical, honest, moral, respectful, responsible, and trustworthy—is the ultimate regimen in building strong, positive moral character.

Honor is in the DNA of leaders of character.

CHAPTER 28

Humility

Humility is a quality projected by a person lacking in arrogance or conceit. It is found in people who maintain a modest opinion or estimate of their own significance, regardless of their position. A leader of character's humility is anchored in compassion and service to others instead of self. Humility is required for any leader to sacrifice his or her own needs in favor of the needs of others.

> Humility is not thinking less of yourself; it's thinking of yourself less.
> —C. S. Lewis, Christian novelist, poet, academic, literary critic, and theologian

> Humility is the foundation of all the other virtues hence, in the soul in which this virtue does not exist, there cannot be any other virtue except in mere appearance.
> —St. Augustine, bishop of Hippo Regius

Humility is buoyed to compassion, appreciation, and respect for others.

The opposite of humility—arrogance—is especially detrimental to leaders because nobody likes arrogance. Arrogant people even dislike other arrogant people. Furthermore, people will be on the lookout for ways or opportunities to sabotage or bring an arrogant person down to earth, and at minimum, people will not assist or follow anyone they consider conceited, egotistical, or haughty. Arrogance has no place in character-based leadership because we are here to serve others, and we just cannot be conceited if we live by that concept.

The following quotes illustrate the importance of humility:

> Humility is a great quality of leadership which derives respect.
> —Yousef Munayyer, Palestinian American writer and political analyst

Humility engenders respect.

> The first test of a truly great man is his humility.
> —John Ruskin, Victorian era art critic, social thinker, and philanthropist

Because influence and power are closely related, leaders must be wary to not allow power to go to their head and produce arrogance. Many leaders fall into the trap, and the result is always a decrease in their influence or complete failure as a leader. Since leaders of character intend to make the world a better place, humility is a mandatory asset.

Humility is a leader's safeguard against arrogance and the damage it causes.

CHAPTER 29

Integrity

Integrity is a person's level of achievement at adhering to, upholding, and living by moral and virtuous principles and values every day and in every situation. It is a person's devotion and faithfulness to their principles, values, and moral character. Integrity is the measure of how well leaders live by and espouse the foundational principles of leaders of character every day, in every situation, and in every role we play throughout our lives.

> The supreme quality for leadership is unquestionably
> integrity. Without it, no real success is possible, no
> matter whether it is on a section gang, a football field,
> in an army, or in an office.
> —Dwight D. Eisenhower, thirty-fourth president of
> the United States

Integrity is a primary indicator of strength of character.

Integrity seems to be a difficult concept for people to fully comprehend. It is most often defined as what you do when nobody is looking, but that is really honor. Integrity is also likely a victim of semantic stretch from misuse and overuse like the word *leadership* is. Such a ubiquitous misunderstanding warrants a deeper look for clarity's sake.

The non-character-related definition of the word *integrity* is "being whole and undivided or unbroken—complete." Accordingly, the character-related definition then is "whole, unbroken, and complete in all aspects of moral character such as compassion, honor, honesty, trustworthiness, respect, and morality." Therefore, having integrity means maintaining the same authenticity, compassion, honesty, honor, morality, ethics, respect, and trustworthiness every day, in every situation, and in every role. It means our words and actions always, in every situation no matter the circumstances, match the kind of person we profess to be and the kind of person others think we are—our character matches our words, persona, reputation, behavior, etc.

A leader with integrity is the same person everywhere, every day, and in every situation.

A person with integrity is the same person, behaving the same way, speaking the same way, abiding by the same moral and ethical standards, with the same honesty, honor, and respect for others whether they are in the middle of nowhere at 3:00 a.m. and nobody is around for miles, or sitting in church with their family, or out partying with friends on Saturday night.

Having integrity means being the same person, maintaining the same honesty, honor, morality, respect,

trustworthiness, and values, no matter what the situation or circumstances.

Our integrity is constantly on display for others in all of our actions, behaviors, and choices. Our true integrity, just like our true character, cannot be masked or hidden in the long term; it will always show through eventually. Leaders are always onstage, always being critiqued and evaluated, so a lot of thought and care has to be given to developing and maintaining the kind of integrity that is expected of a leader—it has to be by intention.

> Waste no more time arguing about what a good man
> should be. Be one.
> —Marcus Aurelius, Roman emperor from
> AD 161 to 180

Leaders must always keep in mind that if integrity is ever sacrificed, lost, or severely damaged, it can never be fully regained or repaired. People may be able to say they forgive a loss of integrity, but they will not forget if their perception of someone's integrity is shattered. Still, many well-known people have sacrificed their integrity and still accomplished great things, so the question arises, Why worry about it?

Sadly, with the number of people in the news sacrificing their integrity, the real damage is in the likelihood that some, especially young people, might believe that integrity is not important. However, we have to be very aware that those who publically destroy their integrity are a microscopic proportion of the total, and they are not at all relevant in normal, everyday life where 99.99 percent of us live. The vast majority of people do maintain their integrity, but never end up on the news because living with integrity is not news—acting the right way and doing the right thing is simply not newsworthy. In fact, a great test for deciding whether we should do something is found in answering the question, Would I maintain my integrity if I do this and it ends up on the front page of the newspaper? The answer is a simple yes or no.

Furthermore, while it might appear that integrity was not important to those successful people who lost it but still accomplished something, what more might they have accomplished if they had maintained their integrity? Also, we cannot know how much disgust, shame, and embarrassment they and their families endure when they should be proud of their accomplishments. It would have to be hard looking in the mirror every day knowing how much better they could feel about themselves in the end if they had just maintained their integrity. We can make no mistake; integrity is important to everyone, regardless of the level of success, and especially to those who have lost it.

The following quote sums up the critical value of integrity for all of us.

> You cannot consistently perform in a manner that is inconsistent with the way you view yourself.
> —Zig Ziglar, author, salesman, and motivational speaker

Our conscience and subconscious minds will ultimately guide us to act the way we really see ourselves. We cannot help it; we will act like the kind of people that we see ourselves as. Our true inner selves will always ultimately match our outer personas. This fact also means that we can become the kind of people we want to become; there is no part of us or our character that cannot be changed. While there are many influences from the outside world that can impact our integrity if we let it happen, it is still always fully under our own control. If we break our integrity, it will be by choice; maintaining it is also by choice.

> Your name and your integrity are the only two things
> that cannot be taken away from you ... you can only
> give your integrity away.
> —General Peter Pace, USMC, sixteenth chairman of
> the Joint Chiefs of Staff

We are each in complete control of our own integrity. We alone have the ability to make the choices to maintain it or give it away—nobody can take it from us.

CHAPTER 30

Intuition

Intuition is the ability to know something without being conscious of how we know it or knowing the answer without being able to fully explain how we know. It is also thought of as instinct, insight, a hunch, or a gut feeling. It is the ability to understand something without consciously thinking and reasoning.

Intuition and *instinct* are abstract concepts and difficult to explain. The following quotes help shed light on the subject:

> Intuition comes very close to clairvoyance; it appears to be the extrasensory perception of reality.
> —Alexis Carrel, Nobel Prize-winning surgeon and biologist

> Intuition is a spiritual faculty and does not explain, but simply points the way.
> —Florence Scovel Shinn, artist, spiritual teacher, and metaphysical writer

> Faith is a passionate intuition.
> —William Wordsworth, English romantic poet

Good instincts usually tell you what to do long before
your head has figured it out.
—Michael Burke, author

Instinct is untaught ability.
—Alexander Bain, Scottish philosopher and
educationalist

Intuition is our subconscious decision-making assistant. While our
conscious minds are trying to grasp the situation, our subconscious
intuition or instinct is also reading the situation and developing a plan
of attack all on its own. Real benefit comes from the ability to get the
two to work together by consciously using intuition. Effectiveness and
accuracy of decisions and actions can be improved by developing and
tapping into this very powerful human ability.

Intuition will tell the thinking mind where to look
next.
—Jonas Salk, American medical researcher

Trusting our intuition often saves us from disaster.
—Anne Wilson Schaef, lecturer, consultant, author

The only real valuable thing is intuition.
—Albert Einstein, German theoretical physicist

Intuition comes from many places including knowledge, real-world
experience, common sense, wisdom, and from a deep understanding
of people. The more we do something, the more tacit knowledge we
develop, and in turn, the more intuition or instinct we develop.

Everyone has heard about "women's intuition." There is likely some credence to women having better intuition than men because women are more naturally in tune with people's emotions and relationships than men are. This trait likely aids women's intuition; however, anyone can develop and make use of intuition by developing knowledge and experience and practicing listening to that inner voice.

> Common sense is instinct, and enough of it is genius.
> —Josh Billings (the pen name of humorist Henry
> Wheeler Shaw)

Sometimes our instinct has a better grip on reality than we do.

CHAPTER 31

Knowledge

Knowledge is information, ideas, facts, subjects, truths, and data that we possess in our minds. It is the condition of consciously learning and knowing facts. Knowledge is simply what and how much we know.

Leaders are most effective if considered smart, intelligent, sharp, and bright. Although the leader does not have to be the smartest, most intelligent, or sharpest, his or her credibility and influence are enhanced with an elevated level of knowledge. Therefore, successful leaders commit a lot of time and effort to learning—great leaders are insatiable lifelong learners.

> An investment in knowledge pays the best interest.
> —Benjamin Franklin, founding father of the United
> States, inventor, and social entrepreneur

The more knowledge we possess, the greater the ultimate return.

Knowledge is one of the easiest of the elements to develop because we are all quite capable of learning and gaining real-world experience in a multitude of subjects. In fact, there is no end to what we can learn, and there will always be more to learn. The old saying is true: "The more you learn, the dumber you get," because the more you learn, the more you find out you don't know.

> To know, is to know that you know nothing. That is
> the meaning of true knowledge.
> —Socrates, (469-399 BC) classical Greek philosopher

> And what, Socrates, is the food of the soul? Surely, I
> said, knowledge is the food of the soul.
> —Plato, classical Greek philosopher

Knowledge is developed through education and experience. Formal education takes long-term commitment, the perseverance to stick with it even through the tough times, and the self-discipline to put education ahead of many other much more fun activities. Experience comes through actively seeking and pursuing opportunities to get into positions that offer a chance to gain valuable firsthand experiences.

Institutional or formal education is one route to education, but there are a multitude of other ways. With the Internet, there is likely no subject on earth we cannot learn about, and of course one of the oldest ways of learning is also still very viable—reading. Listening to audio books while traveling is very effective as well. Common sense is developed by putting knowledge to work in the real world, and there are countless opportunities and means to do that every day, so there is no excuse for leaders to not be continuously learning.

Everyone has the ability to develop any amount of knowledge desired—with enough intention and commitment.

CHAPTER 32

Locus of Control

Locus of control is a person's belief or point of view as to how much control he or she has over the events that impact his or her life. People generally fall into one of two points of view: internal locus of control or external locus of control. People with an *internal locus of control* believe the events in their lives are a result or reflection of their own choices, decisions, or actions. People with an *external locus of control* believe that events in their lives are guided by (or the result of) forces, people, or factors outside of themselves in the external world that they cannot control.

People with an internal locus of control believe we are responsible for what happens to us, we are in control of our own destiny, and we are solely responsible for our own success—or failure. This kind of person is self-reliant, independent, learns from mistakes, and makes no excuses for failure—all essential skills and mind-set for leaders.

Most great leaders and successful people have an internal locus of control.

The opposite is someone with an external locus of control. Their problems are not of their own making. They do not truly feel they are able to control the events in their lives or the random things that happen to them; they believe their problems are mostly caused by others or forces from the outside world. The following quote from Henry Ford illustrates the problem with having an external locus of control.

> If you think you can do it, or you think you can't do it, you are right.
> —Henry Ford, American industrialist, founder of Ford Motor Company

For years, researchers have attempted to identify the ingredients or secrets of success in hopes of creating a recipe or road map that everyone could follow. The studies have pretty much failed because no two successful people achieved success exactly the same way or followed the exact same route or recipe. However, there are a few traits that are shared by most successful people—traits that we can emulate and adopt. One trait nearly every successful person has is an internal locus of control. Intuitively, it is easy to understand because nobody hands out success and there's nobody in charge of it; we have to intentionally seek and earn it ourselves. Being a great leader is exactly the same. It has to be sought and earned, so an internal locus of control is imperative.

Maintaining an internal locus of control is maintaining control of your own character and destiny.

A concept that is directly connected with locus of control is individual motivation: how a person is motivated. Like locus of control, people are generally divided into two groups: *intrinsically motivated* or *extrinsically motivated*. Intrinsic motivation means the motivation comes from inside; extrinsic from the outside. Intrinsically motivated people are driven to achieve by an internal drive or desire. Extrinsically motivated people are moved by external motivators such as rewards or recognition. Intrinsic motivation is substantially more powerful than extrinsic motivation because extrinsic motivation disappears once the reward is gained or removed.

Leaders cannot be authentic if leading for the rewards, so the desire to be a leader is always intrinsic. Leaders have, or they develop, an innate desire or drive to step up and lead. Leaders of character lead simply because of the personal satisfaction that comes from working to make the world a better place—that is intrinsic motivation.

Leaders of character are intrinsically motivated because the reward is simply the personal satisfaction from helping make the world a better place.

CHAPTER 33

Morality and Ethics

Morality is the measure of how moral a person is, or how well a person abides by his or her morals. It is the level to which a person conforms to right, good, and virtuous behavior. *Morals* are personal principles and standards of what is right and wrong; good and bad; virtue and vice. Moral behavior is right, good, and virtuous behavior.

Morality is demonstrated by how dearly we live every day and publically display behavior and actions that are right, good, and virtuous.

Ethics are public standards and rules of conduct defining right and wrong, and good and bad behavior. Being *ethical* or maintaining *ethical behavior* is doing and behaving right and good.

Morals and *ethics* are often used synonymously; however, they differ in that morals are more about beliefs held in the heart and gut that guide our actions, whereas ethics are more about actions or rules of social or public behavior. Morals are principles and virtues we hold ourselves accountable for, and ethics are principles and virtues the civilized world holds us accountable for. Accordingly, morals can be thought of as internal ethics, and ethics as visible morals.

Morality and ethics are also often considered in concert with religion; however, while most religions promote morality and ethical behavior, neither morality nor ethics are the domain of any religion, and neither is connected to or dependent upon any religious beliefs. That said, what many people consider moral and ethical is determined or guided by their religious faith; however, many behaviors are designated differently, and even oppositely, by different or opposing faiths. For instance, what may be considered moral and ethical by one faith may be completely immoral and unethical in the eyes of another. This lack of universal agreement between religions insures that morality cannot rely solely on religion; therefore, the quandary of defining right and wrong must instead be dealt with by society as a whole in order to create accepted definitions of moral and ethical behavior that are then prescribed for everyone, regardless of religious beliefs.

> Morality is of the highest importance—but for us, not
> for God.
> —Albert Einstein, German theoretical physicist

Moral and ethical behaviors are determined by society because the behavior of its individuals is ultimately about survival of civilized human society. The criteria used to decide what is moral and ethical behavior is how a behavior impacts a human's most basic need to survive and desire to prosper and be happy. When society is developing an opinion on moral or ethical questions, the collective is simply trying to decide, en masse, if the behavior harms or hinders humanity's need to survive and desire to prosper and be happy.

For example, someone stealing our belongings would harm our basic need to survive as well as our prosperity and happiness, so society long ago deemed stealing immoral and unethical. Immoral or unethical behaviors that rise to a significant enough level of damage, like stealing, are considered so immoral and unethical by society that laws are created against such behaviors.

It must be noted however that morals and ethics are not dependent upon, or even connected to, any laws either. Laws are meant mostly to protect people and their property from harm or unjust actions, so laws cannot cover every moral or ethical issue. In fact, many immoral and unethical actions are quite legal, and some moral and ethical actions are illegal. Laws are created by imperfect humans who are influenced by numerous factors like religion or public opinion, so laws are also imperfect—sometimes very imperfect!

> Ethics is knowing the difference between what you
> have a right to do and what is right to do.
> —Potter Stewart, US Supreme Court justice

To understand why some actions are deemed immoral, or to determine if an action would be immoral, we can simply answer this question: What if everyone did it? Insert any questionable action or behavior and honestly contemplate the long-term answer to that question. Take, for example, cheating on tests in school. There is no gray area, weasel room, or degrees of severity when cheating—we either are cheating, or we are not cheating. So, if all of a sudden it was not wrong, immoral, and unethical to cheat, what would the eventual result be?

Well, envision what it would be like if all doctors cheated on every test all the way through medical school; airline pilots through flight school; airplane manufacturers, teachers, automobile manufacturers, lawyers, police, fire fighters, builders, preachers, soldiers, mayors, governors, senators, the president, and on and on. Add to the mental picture the other behaviors that would also result from the cheating in terms of retaliation, defense, or retribution? You would not have to envision very far into the future to realize that complete chaos would result, and at some point, an absolute breakdown of civilized society. In fact, if we kept going with this scenario, we could easily go all the way to the end of civilization—all because cheating was not wrong, immoral, or unethical!

Moral and ethical behavior is what holds our world together.

A serious problem that leaders must be very attuned to is what it is that makes usually moral and ethical people act immorally or unethically, sometimes to the point of completely ruining their life. Why do good people do bad things occasionally? Why do people who seem to have everything going for them do things that tear their life apart and hurt those who are closest to them, like family and friends? Hardly a week goes by that we do not hear about some high-profile, successful, or public person, who seemed to have a life most anyone else would love to have, get caught up in some kind of ethical or moral scandal. While we cannot truly understand them and their specific situations, the proliferation of the problem must make us aware that we might also be capable of making the same mistakes. Therefore, understanding what might have caused their destructive behavior could help us keep from following the same path.

We may never truly understand what makes some people do some of the stupid things they do; however, David DeSteno and Piercarlo Valdesolo, in their book *Out of Character*,[10] offer a plausible explanation. In the book, they suggest that "there lurks in all of us the potential to lie, cheat, steal, and sin, no matter how good a person we believe ourselves to be." All of us! They further propose that our behavior and decisions may not be what we morally intend, but are instead a product of "dueling forces" in our minds and psyches trying to adjust to our needs, situations, and priorities. The typical picture we have of our morality is an angel on one shoulder and the devil on the other, each doing their best to influence us to their way.

The authors paint an alternative picture of our morality based on Aesop's fable, "The Ant and the Grasshopper," where our morals are not on a scale of good on one end and bad on the other. Instead, it's more of a tug-of-war between the grasshopper and ant from the fable. The grasshopper wants to have fun right now—immediate pleasure and rewards, instant gratification, and very little thought to the future— whereas the ant wants to take care of the future before having fun and will forgo instant gratification in the interest of future gratification and long-term concern for the colony or family.

The ant is all about long-term survival, and the grasshopper is all about taking care of immediate wants and needs. These dueling forces are

---

[10] DeSteno, David and Piercarlo Valdesolo. *Out of Character*. New York: Crown Publishing Group. 2011. Print.

both actually very powerful evolutionary behaviors that have been with us since the dawn of mankind. And both are looking out for our best interests—just in different time frames. The grasshopper appears to be the one who causes the trouble, so it would seem the best thing to do is consciously follow the ant—but it is not that simple. Willpower cannot control either of the forces for long. We all naturally care about the colony (i.e., our family or social world), but we also care about our individual wants and needs. Balancing the two is very tricky because our short-term interests or desires very often conflict with our long-term responsibilities. When the wrong one of these dueling forces wins at the wrong time, that's when usually moral and ethical people do immoral and unethical things.

Every leader must always remain vigilant of these human weaknesses not only in our own self, but in others as well in order to guard against entrapment in someone else's poor choices or ethical failures—guilt by association is real. Leaders of character gladly accept living to higher-than-average moral standards and expectations; it is just one of the prices of leadership. Moreover, the more influential a leader becomes, the higher the standards and expectations that are placed upon us. This assertion is supported by the following quote from one of America's founding fathers.

> Because power corrupts, society's demands for moral
> authority and character increase as the importance of
> the position increases.
> —John Adams, American founding father and the
> second president of the United States

Luckily, we have an internal innate mechanism that helps to guide us in maintaining our morality: our conscience or moral compass. Our moral compass is an inner voice that directs us toward moral and ethical behavior like a magnetic compass guides towards the north. The guilt we feel when we stray from our true north moral compass is a very powerful motivator to help get us back on track.

Still another related motivating mechanism is the impact our moral fabric has on our entire life. Our moral fabric is our morality across every aspect of our lives, including all of the different roles we play (father, mother, brother, sister, husband, wife, coworker, peer, friend, etc.). No one role can be isolated from another when it comes to our morality; moral or immoral behavior in any one role directly impacts all of our roles because neither our subconscious nor our conscience differentiates between roles. While we might be able to hide immoral or unethical behavior from the outside world, we can never hide it from our subconscious or our conscience.

So leaders who listen to their moral compasses and maintain a strong moral fabric increase their chances of success and absolutely insure greater peace of mind.

The leader's highest duty is to set the morality and ethical standards in stone, then model them explicitly. If the leader doesn't, who will?

CHAPTER 34

Optimism

Optimism is a person's disposition that is always hopeful, sees the best in all situations, and expects positive and favorable outcomes in everything. Optimists see the glass half full where their opposites, pessimists, see the glass as half empty.

Like attitude, optimism is a state-of-mind trait because it is impacted by, and illustrative of, a person's emotional, cognitive, and mental state. While we do have significant ability to consciously determine our level of optimism, it is still impacted by a number of factors beyond our control. Therefore, again, the best strategy to develop our optimism is a focus on our overall character development; stronger, more positive character will result in stronger, more positive optimism.

Optimism is important for leaders because it creates hope in followers. Hope is a powerful motivator for people. As long as there is hope, people are capable of phenomenal feats; without hope, people will not even try. Besides hope, optimism is also positive energy as opposed to pessimism being negative energy. People are naturally drawn to optimism and positive energy because of the contagiousness.

Optimism and hope are jet fuel for our capabilities.

Following are several quotes from people who should certainly know the importance of optimism:

Believe you can and you're halfway there.
—Theodore Roosevelt, twenty-sixth president of the United States

What I've really learned over time is that optimism is a very, very important part of leadership.
—Bob Iger, CEO of Walt Disney Company

Optimism is the faith that leads to achievement. Nothing can be done without hope and confidence.
—Helen Keller, deaf and blind author, activist, and lecturer

Optimism is the madness of insisting that all is well when we are miserable.
—Voltaire, French Enlightenment writer and philosopher

Pessimism leads to weakness, optimism to power.
—William James, psychologist and philosopher

Perpetual optimism is a force multiplier.
—General Colin Powell, American statesman and retired four-star Army general

General Powell's quote means that optimism will increase the capability of the troops or followers. Lasting optimism increases productivity, or output per person, in business just as it will increase a leader's influence. Leaders can increase their influence and impact simply by being perpetual optimism producers.

Optimism is a leader's influence multiplier.

CHAPTER 35

Passion

Passion is a person's strong, deep, intense internal conviction, devotion, or enthusiasm for an activity, object, or concept. It is a force that drives people to reach exaggerated achievements. For leaders of character, passion is an inflated level of conviction and enthusiasm for what we believe in, what we do, and all that we represent.

Passion is a supercharged motivational force.

A leader's passion inspires followers, a fact touted by most experienced leaders and authors as critical to a leader's impact. Passion is positive emotion, and people are moved much more by positive emotions than even words or actions. Passion draws people in and lifts up their spirit.

Passion is also extremely contagious and a powerful attractant. People are supernaturally drawn to someone who is very passionate about something that they also care about. For example, the phenomenal growth of the Methodist church in the 1700s is largely credited to the passion of one man: John Wesley. The reason for the phenomenon is illustrated in his answer when asked why so many people came to hear him preach. In answering, he said, "I set myself on fire and people come

135

to watch me burn." What he meant was he let his passion loose and it attracted countless followers.

The following quotes illustrate the power of feelings versus words and actions.

> I've learned that people will forget what you said,
> people will forget what you did, but people will never
> forget how you made them feel.
> —Maya Angelou, American author and poet

> They may forget what you said, but they will never
> forget how you made them feel.
> —Carl W. Buechner, Presbyterian minister and
> author

The greatest passion is from a natural love or enthusiasm, but passion is not genetic, no one is born passionate about anything. As we go through life, we are drawn to what we are most interested in, and our excitement and enthusiasm begin to grow. Everyone can be passionate about something; the trick is finding it. Anyone reading this book has an interest in leadership, indicating at least a seed of enthusiasm. Developing passion out of that seed is what great leaders who know the power of passion do. The way to truly make a huge impact is to be completely committed, and the only way to be completely committed is to be passionate.

A leader's ultimate impact on the world will be proportional to his or her passion.

Leaders must be aware that passion, no matter how strong, comes and goes, or rises and falls like the tides of the ocean. Passion varies because it is affected by numerous influences like our life situation or circumstances, responsibilities, other duties that require our attention, and so on. Nobody, not even the most passionate, maintains a steady high level of passion continuously for extended periods of time. This variation is actually beneficial because if we were able to maintain a permanent high level of passion, it would become commonplace and normal everyday behavior, thereby losing its positive energy and its supercharged motivational power. Our challenge is to continue to persevere through the lulls and dips in passion. Perseverance, commitment, and discipline come into synergistic play with passion during these lulls.

> The most powerful weapon on earth is the human soul on fire.
> —Field Marshal Ferdinand Foch, French soldier, military theorist, and First World War hero

Passion is the power driving every great leader's accomplishments.

CHAPTER 36

People Skills

Everyone wants to feel important, special, and respected—everyone! Everyone also wants personal attention and to be treated as individuals. It is the leader's responsibility to always keep these basic human demands in mind.

People skills are a person's ability to interact and communicate with other people. People skills also include connecting skills, interpersonal skills, networking skills, and social skills. People skills include the ability to:

- strike up and carry on conversations and small talk, even with strangers.
- intentionally meet new people, get to know them, and develop relationships and friendships.
- actively listen.
- persuade or negotiate with no offense or resentment.
- read and interpret people's body language and emotions.
- make people comfortable in uncomfortable situations.
- make people feel good about themselves and about you.
- draw people in and get them involved in conversations or activities.

Since leadership is about personal relationships, people skills are critically important to leaders.

> The most important single ingredient in the formula of success is knowing how to get along with people.
> —Theodore Roosevelt, twenty-sixth president of the United States

People skills seem to be the domain of only those who are naturally gregarious, extroverted, or natural social butterflies. It seems the majority of people are generally paralyzed when faced with a socializing situation in a room full of strangers. This socializing fear comes from the same place that the fear of public speaking arises, and we know that is most people's number one fear (even greater than the fear of death). Social fear is fear of humiliation, failure, or rejection, and it is difficult to overcome. However, people skills and the ability to socialize, network, and small talk are learnable skills that anyone can develop. In fact, it is a leader's responsibility to develop people skills in order to help followers be more comfortable in the social aspects of leadership.

People skills are developed through lots of practice in social events, but there is also a lot of benefit in studying and reading about such topics as body language, interpersonal, cross-gender and multicultural communications, psychology, relationships, and sociology. There are even books on mingling, networking, small talk, and how to have social conversations. The word *networking* has a sort of negative connotation, but networking and connecting are simply socializing with intent to meet new people. Networking and connecting is the skill, art, and science of meeting people, being liked, and developing long-lasting mutually beneficial relationships—almost the same as leadership.

> The more people you know, and who know you in
> a positive way, the more successful you will be at
> anything you attempt.
> —Brian Tracy, self-help author and motivational
> speaker

Networking, connecting, and socializing are learnable skills, or more succinctly, a series of skills. Learning these skills is an entire subject in itself, much too vast to cover in depth here, but following are a few key hints from Keith Ferrazzi's book, *Never Eat Alone.*[11]

- Meet people to help them, not so they can help you. Real networking is working hard to give more than you get.
- Go public. Join and get involved in public clubs or organizations (Chamber, Rotary, Lions, etc.). This offers the opportunity to socialize in controlled settings.
- Be proactive. Begin getting to know people now.
- Develop audacity. Audacity will be a huge help in most everything we do, especially networking. It is not being afraid to meet people, to put ourselves out there open to ridicule or criticism.
- Do the homework. Before meeting someone new or going to a social event, learn all you can about them or who might be at the event. The more you know, the more familiar they will be, so the easier it will be to have a conversation with them.
- Be passionate about numerous things (i.e., family, job, school, nonprofits, charities, hobbies, church, golf, hunting, fishing,

---

[11] Ferrazzi, Keith with Tal Raz. *Never Eat Alone*. New York: Doubleday. 2005. Print.

food, wine, etc.) and be open to sharing your passions with others. This shows we are human and interesting, and others will follow suit and be energized by our passion.

- Learn how to "small talk." This is the ability to carry on a civil conversation about everyday topics. To help develop small-talk skills, learn to have something to talk about. Good subjects to talk about include current events, news, wine, food, nonprofits, travel, restaurants, etc. Learn to ask sincere probing questions, because the greatest subject in the world is the person we are talking to.
- Lighten up. Don't be too serious. Humor is always good, especially self-deprecating humor.
- Learn to read and use nonverbal language.
- Remember that no one is perfect; in fact, pointing out our own imperfections is one of the greatest strategies to put others at ease.

You can make more friends in two months by becoming really interested in other people than you can in two years by trying to get other people interested in you. Which is just another way of saying that the way to make a friend is to be one.
—Dale Carnegie (1888-1955), author of *How to Win Friends and Influence People*, and the founding father of modern self-improvement

Since leadership is about personal interactions, expert people skills will smooth a leader's road to success.

CHAPTER 37

Perseverance

Perseverance is a person's persistent, dogged, and steadfast determination to follow a course of action or pursuit of a purpose regardless of difficulties. Persevering is continuing on course in spite of resisting forces, obstacles, opposition, or discouragement. For leaders, it is a tenacious drive and determination to keep on going and advancing no matter the hurdles and difficulty.

Perseverance encompasses several other vital leadership and success traits or habits such as

- Dedication: deep loyalty and commitment
- Devotion: intense allegiance and attachment
- Doggedness: obstinate determination
- Drive: relentless, enthusiastic internal obligation or compulsion
- Endurance: capacity to withstand an unpleasant process
- Grit: toughness and resilience in the face of difficult or painful circumstances
- Persistence: a strong commitment to continue
- Tenacity: stubborn, firm, and tough persistence

Mankind's greatest achievements come only through significant strength-of-mind traits like perseverance, dedication, devotion, doggedness, drive, grit, persistence, and tenacity. The greatest achievements require an abundance of each.

Perseverance and all of the perseverance traits are strength-of-mind traits because they illustrate the sturdiness, tenacity, and vigor of our mental and cognitive profile on a level generally beyond our conscious understanding. Perseverance, persistence, tenacity, and the other traits indicate the toughness or grittiness of our mind—the tougher our mind, the more perseverance we have. Our mind's toughness is determined by numerous factors such as how resolute or committed we are to what we are doing, how passionate we are about it, how competent we are, how confident we are in our abilities, and numerous other environmental, personal, and physiological factors. However, even though much of this is going on outside of our consciousness, we do have some ability to consciously develop and strengthen our perseverance. As usual, the best strategy is a focus on character development. A stronger, more positive and more virtuous character will result in stronger perseverance, persistence, determination, tenacity, and all of the other perseverance traits.

> Grit is passion and perseverance for very long-term goals.
> —Angela Lee Duckworth, PhD psychologist and success researcher

Anyone who has ever accomplished anything of significance will attest to the importance of all of the perseverance traits. Significant accomplishment, achievement, or success is never easy for anyone, so the most successful people are almost always the most dedicated, persistent, gritty, and driven. Leaders do not necessarily have to be the most persistent or the grittiest, but they better be close to it if a great impact is the goal.

The importance of perseverance traits is highlighted well in the following quotes:

> Endurance is one of the most difficult disciplines,
> but it is to the one who endures that the final victory
> comes.
> —Buddha, spiritual teacher and founder of Buddhism

> Perseverance is a great element of success. If you only
> knock long enough and loud enough at the gate, you
> are sure to wake up somebody.
> —Henry Wadsworth Longfellow, American poet and
> educator

> People of mediocre ability sometimes achieve
> outstanding success because they don't know
> when to quit. Most men succeed because they are
> determined to.
> —George E. Allen, football coach

> I do not think there is any other quality so essential to
> success of any kind as the quality of perseverance. It
> overcomes almost everything, even nature.
> —John D. Rockefeller, American industrialist and
> philanthropist

Nothing in this world can take the place of persistence. Talent will not; nothing is more common than unsuccessful people with talent. Genius will not; unrewarded genius is almost a proverb. Education will not; the world is full of educated derelicts. Persistence and determination alone are omnipotent. The slogan "press on" has solved and always will solve the problems of the human race.

—Calvin Coolidge, thirtieth president of the United States

Good luck is another name for tenacity of purpose.

—Ralph Waldo Emerson, American essayist, lecturer, and poet

It's not that I'm so smart; it's just that I stay with problems longer.

—Albert Einstein, German theoretical physicist

Nothing of great significance was ever achieved without great perseverance!

Another especially important concept encompassed within perseverance is *work ethic*. Work ethic is a person's belief in the value of hard work and in giving 100 percent (or more) of the effort a job, assignment, or activity requires. A great work ethic is the opposite of lazy or apathetic. A person with a good work ethic believes in giving his or her best in their work or job. Today's more urban, high tech, and automated world seems to be deteriorating work ethic, but that may not be true; hard work today may not always entail sweat and strenuous manual labor as in the agricultural or industrial age. The knowledge-based economy requires just as great a work ethic to be successful, but it is much more about mental work than physical. So, while people aren't growing up as much on farms today where hard work ethic is best taught, the new generations are forced to develop a work ethic in new ways—if they do not, the world, and success, will leave them behind. A great work ethic is just as vital today as ever.

For leaders, laziness and apathy are lethal.

Since the leader's duty is to set the example, leaders must have a good work ethic. The leader has to be the first one there and the last one to leave at minimum. The leader also cannot be timid about jumping in and doing whatever work needs to be done.

The shortage of the perseverance traits, and the damage caused by the scarcity, is illustrated in high school and college dropout rates. Anyone who has finished high school, and especially anyone who has completed college, certainly knows that the main key to success is tenacity and dedication, as well as a heaping of the other perseverance traits. Earning a degree is a long-term process that requires lots of hours and work, much of which is absolutely no fun at all. A lot of recreation and socializing with friends and family must be sacrificed to be successful in school, especially college. Consequently, people with little grit or a weak work ethic have an extremely difficult time succeeding through high school or college. Because of this, an earned diploma or degree does not illustrate intelligence as much as it shows that the graduate has the perseverance, grit, work ethic, and all of the other requirements to complete a long-term difficult process—valuable traits to every employer.

The question should then be asked, How can we strengthen our perseverance traits? The first strategy is in developing character, but following are some additional helpful practices:

- Set goals; write them down and revisit them often. We get significant motivation from striving to reach a specific goal or target.
- Find what you are passionate about and pursue it.
- Study the lives of successful people to find out how much they had to persevere. Knowing how much our heroes had to persist is very motivational.
- Enlist others to help and ask them to push you. We are motivated to not let others down.
- Plan ahead. We are more motivated to keep going if we know where we are going.
- Develop and implement strategies that motivate you (i.e., if you work better early in the morning, get up early every day).
- Always overestimate how long and how difficult the task is going to be. We are motivated by the pleasant realization that it is easier or that we are going finish sooner than expected.
- Make sure you know why you are doing whatever it is you're doing; know what your purpose is.

Perseverance traits only see us through the tough times that we make it through.

CHAPTER 38

Professionalism

Professionalism is the quality or level of class in how people present themselves when interacting with others. Professionalism is about a person presenting a polished professional image and presence and it includes attire/clothing, attitude, behavior/conduct, body language, communications skills, customs, decorum, etiquette, friends/associates, language, manners, reputation, style, and other components. For leaders, the value of professionalism, or having a professional image, is increased influence through an increase in credibility and respect from others. Looking, feeling, and acting professional also develops and projects other beneficial attributes such as charisma, confidence, and competence.

Professionalism is a variable, relative, and situation-defined quality depending on location, culture, expectations, and other factors. Regardless of our individual situation, most of us know professionalism when we see it—and when we do not. Though the entire discipline of professionalism is much too vast to explore in detail here, following is a short discussion of some of the more important components of a professional image.

Attire/Clothing: Like it or not, people judge, and are judged, by looks, which means we all judge each other by how we dress; by the clothes we wear, all the way down to our shoes and socks. The power of first impressions is well known, and the power of attire on those first impressions is monumental. Therefore, leaders follow a fairly strict code for wearing appropriate clothing in all social situations. If going into a new situation where the exact level of dress is unknown, a good rule of thumb is to dress one level above the expected dress code. In creating a professional image, it is much better to be overdressed than underdressed. An in-depth knowledge of professional style and attire is invaluable.

Men should learn to be comfortable in a tie. Although dress codes may be trending towards more casual attire, ties are very professional and still make a good impression. A side benefit from wearing a tie is men seem to automatically act and carry ourselves more professionally when wearing one.

> Great men are seldom over-scrupulous in the
> arrangement of their attire.
> —Charles Dickens, English author and social critic

Attitude is so important that it is one of the elements. For leaders, a professional attitude is maintaining a sense of formality and decorum. A professional demeanor is friendly, composed, and level-headed.

Behavior/Conduct: This is also so important that is it one of elements. Professionals act mature and polished, and project a sense of style and class. This is one of the more defining aspects of professionalism. Mature behavior is simply acting appropriately for the given situation. Polished behavior is appearing comfortable and at ease regardless of the situation. Projecting a sense of style and class comes from acting with sophistication and appropriately in any given situation. Poor, crude, or boorish behavior has no place in a professional image.

Professional leaders act the right way at the right time.

Chivalry: In medieval stories, chivalry was illustrated by a code that knights lived by that demanded generous, just, gracious, courteous, high-minded, noble, and righteous actions and behavior. Though the word *chivalrous* is not used a lot these days, the world would certainly be better off if we honored the knight's code. Of benefit to leaders, because of the rarity of chivalry, being highly chivalrous is a great way for anyone to stand out above the crowd. Leaders illustrate modern chivalry by simply acting like a "lady" or a "gentlemen."

> The institution of chivalry forms one of the most
> remarkable features in the history of the Middle Ages.
> —Horatio Alger, nineteenth-century American author

Chivalry is one of the greatest ways to stand out above the crowd.

Conflict Facilitator: Every leader faces conflict; it is inevitable whenever people are involved. Add in the change that is inherent in leadership, and conflict can be enormous. Most people try to avoid conflict, but conflict has an important role in the advancement of organizations, and even societies. Conflict is the genesis of countless advancements throughout the history of mankind. Extreme discomfort, disagreements, and even quarrels are required sometimes to get complacent people out of their comfort zones in order to open up opportunities for progress. A professional leader knows how to facilitate, manage, and control conflict in order to reap the benefits by guiding it toward beneficial outcomes. In today's world, more and more organizations are realizing the advantages of controlled conflict and discomfort, so the skill of conflict facilitator is becoming a very sought-after skill.

> Difficulties are meant to rouse, not discourage. The
> human spirit is to grow strong by conflict.
> —William Ellery Channing, foremost nineteenth
> century Unitarian preacher

Emotional Stability: Emotional stability is simply maintaining control of our emotions. For leaders, that means maintaining control especially during emotional events or times when others may be losing control of their emotions. Truthfully, professional emotional stability means strict control or elimination of negative emotions such as anger, contempt, embarrassment, envy, grief, or hatred while maintaining positive emotions such as affection, camaraderie, happiness, and love. Emotions cause people to do more damage than any other factor, but damage can be mitigated or prevented completely by someone who has control of their emotions acting as a stabilizing force. It is a leader's professional duty to be a stabilizing emotional force.

> When dealing with people, remember you are not
> dealing with creatures of logic, but creatures of
> emotion.
> —Dale Carnegie (1888-1955), author of *How to Win
> Friends and Influence People,* and the founding father
> of modern self-improvement

Etiquette: Etiquette may seem superficial, but it is one of the more obvious and important activities or places where professionalism is projected (or where its absence is most obvious). People laugh at such rules as which fork to use or how to eat a piece of chicken at a formal dinner; however, there are some very important reasons to be well-versed in the rules of etiquette. Etiquette's role is to smooth social functions and interactions, but there is also a higher order reason for professional decorum. Professional etiquette is akin to an informal civilian version of military ceremony, pageantry, and protocol that builds considerable respect, pride, and tradition in military personnel. Civilian society would certainly benefit from more ceremony and the resulting increase in respect, pride, and tradition as well—that is a benefit of professional etiquette. For leaders, expertise at etiquette rules helps make others more comfortable at social functions, which results in everyone enjoying the experience much more. Etiquette is another of the subjects that is too vast to cover here, but there are plenty of sources available to learn the skill.

> Etiquette is the science of living. It embraces
> everything. It is ethics. It is honor.
> —Emily Post, American etiquette author

Friends/Associates: "Guilt by association" is a hard and true fact of life; consequently, our professional image is significantly impacted by who we are associated with. There is a reason successful people belong to exclusive country clubs and organizations: successful people know the value of being associated with successful people. In fact, sometimes our friends are our worst enemies because they hold us to the lowest standards. Surrounding ourselves with people who hold us to higher standards of professionalism motivates us to reach that standard.

Associate with men of good quality if you esteem your own reputation; for it is better to be alone than in bad company.
—Booker T. Washington, American political leader, teacher, and author

Generosity: Professionals are generous with not only their money and resources, but also their time, assistance, and other support. This is mostly for the great feeling that comes from giving, but also because the old saying is very true: "What goes around comes around." Professional leaders know that the only way to be successful is with the help of countless other people. To gain such help, we must first help countless others.

You can have everything in life that you want if you just give enough other people what they want.
—Zig Ziglar, author, salesman, and motivational speaker

Grooming/Personal Appearance: In conjunction with attire, our personal appearance is a huge part of our first impression on others, as well as a necessity in maintaining long-term relationships. People naturally distance themselves from others who are deficient in any aspect of grooming, especially with issues like lack of cleanliness and bad breath or body odor. Grooming or personal appearance includes hair (combed/brushed, cut, style, and even color); hygiene/cleanliness (very regular showers/baths); teeth (brushed often, cleaned regularly, whitened); breath (mouthwash often, mints, brushing); shaving (often); perfume/cologne, makeup, deodorant, etc. A leader's personal grooming and appearance is the doorway that followers must get past before they will be influenced, however superficial that might seem.

> A respectable appearance is sufficient to make people
> more interested in your soul.
> —Karl Lagerfeld, German designer, artist, and
> photographer

Every leader is first judged by appearance. Care about appearance equals care about other elements in the eyes of others.

Language: It seems that cursing or swearing is more acceptable today; however, cursing is not professional language because it is still very offensive to many people and it is too casual and unsophisticated for a professional environment. Cursing and swearing should be left out of leadership because offending anyone goes directly against what character-based leadership is all about. Professional language is not offensive to anyone.

> The foolish and wicked practice of profane cursing
> and swearing is a vice so mean and low that every
> person of sense and character detests and despises it.
> —George Washington, founding father and first
> president of the United States

Manners: Good manners, civility, and treating people courteously and with respect may seem to also be on the decline in today's more casual anything-goes world, but the decline only makes manners more valuable. Perhaps one of the best ways to identify true professionals is to watch their manners and how they treat others. Being mannerly and courteous means treating others like you like them; it is simple actions like saying thank you, my pleasure, yes ma'am, no ma'am, yes sir, no sir, may I help you, excuse me, I'm sorry, etc. Good manners, civility, respect, and common courtesy must be a part of every leader's professional image.

> Good manners are appreciated as much as bad manners are abhorred.
> —Bryant H. McGill, American editor and author

Quality: Professionals are especially motivated to perform quality work in all they do. In fact, nothing says unprofessional more than shoddy work. It is the same for leaders; shoddy, unprofessional leadership will always end badly. Successful leaders strive for excellence in all they do and work to continuously improve.

> The quality, not the longevity, of one's life is what is important.
> —Martin Luther King Jr., clergyman and civil rights leader

Timeliness: Professionals are very punctual, habitual early arrivers, and at worst, they are adamant about always being on time. Being punctual is a sure sign of professionalism because habitual tardiness screams of disrespect and of poor planning and self-discipline. Timeliness for leaders should not be an issue since one of the main leadership duties of the leader is to be one of the first to arrive and one of the last to leave.

> Punctuality is the politeness of kings.
> —Louis XVIII, king of France from 1814-1824

Work Ethic: Professionals always work hard. Like shoddy work screams unprofessional, apathy and laziness scream it as well. Leaders must always exhibit a strong work ethic and relentlessly do the work that needs to be done, or nobody will.

> If the power to do hard work is not a skill, it's the best possible substitute for it.
> —James A. Garfield, twentieth president of the United States

> There is no substitute for hard work.
> —Thomas A. Edison, prolific inventor and businessman

There are still other aspects of leadership professionalism, but that is the subject of another entire book.

For leaders, a professional image is a significant influence multiplier—an unprofessional image is an even more potent influence eliminator.

CHAPTER 39

Respect

Respect, in a leadership context, should be divided into three separate and disparate aspects: "get," the noun version of respect (getting respect, being respected); "give," the verb version (giving respect, respecting others); and "self," respect for our self. All are vital and equally important to every leader.

Giving respect means honoring others and showing them special appreciation, attention, and esteem. Getting respect means being appreciated, admired, and held in high esteem by others. Self-respect is how highly we regard our own esteem, reputation, value, or standing. For leaders, respect is how highly we regard, appreciate, and honor others (give); how highly others regard and trust us (get); and how much self-respect we display.

A leader must be respected (get) to be successful because nobody will be positively influenced by anyone they have no respect for. And, the old saying is true: "Respect cannot be demanded, it must be earned." One of the most important ways to earn it is to give it. To envision the power of giving respect we can observe what happens when the reverse happens, when people are disrespected. The scene can get very ugly when people feel they are being disrespected. At minimum, they will certainly have no respect for anyone who disrespects them.

> Respect is a two-way street; if you want to get it,
> you've got to give it.
> —R. G. Risch, author

Many people have witnessed the results of disrespect from a boss at work. Subordinates of a disrespectful manager or boss are always less productive and usually do no more work than they have to just to get by. In fact, if the opportunity presents itself, many (maybe most) will jump at the chance to sabotage a disrespectful boss. Being disrespected feels the same as being humiliated; nobody takes kindly to it, and most of us are prone to lashing out against it.

> Without feelings of respect, what is there to
> distinguish men from beasts?
> —Confucius, Chinese teacher and philosopher

Self-respect, or self-esteem, is another of the all-important state-of-mind traits because it is illustrative of a person's emotional, cognitive, and mental state. Unlike some of the other state-of-mind traits, self-respect is more a factor of our subconscious view of our self, rather than just our emotional or mental state. We have the ability to consciously influence and control our self-respect, or at least the outward projection of it, but because so much of what impacts our state of mind is beyond our conscious understanding, the best, and perhaps only, strategy to develop our self-respect is by focusing on character development.

Self-respect, or self-esteem, is simply maintaining and showing pride in our self and our own dignity and worth. Self-respect is impacted by many factors such our upbringing, our environment or surroundings, the people we associate with, the quality of life choices we make, past successes and failures, and our level of honesty, honor, integrity, and morality. Maintaining honesty, honor, integrity, and our morality increases pride in ourselves that translates into self-respect, especially on a powerful subconscious character level. The reverse is also true: weakness in any of these areas results in a decreased level of self-respect.

Self-respect seems to be on shaky ground today, especially with young people; therefore, it is one of a leader's higher-level duties to model and promote it. Leaders can have a considerably positive impact on others simply by displaying exemplary self-respect that others see and emulate. The importance of self-respect is noted in these quotes:

> Respect yourself and others will respect you.
> —Confucius, Chinese teacher and philosopher

> Respect for ourselves guides our morals; respect for others guides our manners.
> —Laurence Sterne, Anglo-Irish novelist and clergyman

> If you want to be respected by others, the great thing is to respect yourself. Only by that, only by self-respect will you compel others to respect you.
> —Fyodor Dostoyevsky, Russian novelist

Respect (get) is earned or decreased in numerous ways. In fact, getting respect is correlated with every other element. An increase or decrease in any of them results in the same with respect. It is obvious that respect is integral with every aspect of leaders of character.

Respect is coupled and correlated with every attribute, practice, and principle of life. None of the other elements matter without respect.

CHAPTER 40

Responsibility/Accountability

Responsibility is being accountable, reliable, and trustworthy to yourself and others for your obligations, standards, duties, and conduct. **Accountability** is being answerable, liable, and responsible for your actions and duties. For leaders, responsibility is an elevated level of reliability, dependability, commitment, and determination to fulfill all duties in all roles. Accountability is accepting our responsibility and the consequences of fulfilling it, or not fulfilling it.

Responsibility and accountability have two facets: internal and external. Internal responsibility and accountability is holding ourselves responsible and accountable for our obligations, standards, duties, and conduct. External responsibility and accountability is the responsibility, duty, and accountability we are given and held to by others.

> The price of greatness is responsibility.
> —Winston Churchill, prime minister of England and statesman

Responsibility is tied to locus of control, the extent to which people believe they control their own lives or what happens to them in their lives. People with an internal locus of control, who believe they are in control of their own lives, are much more likely to be responsible and accountable for their own actions because of their belief that they are in control. People with an external locus of control, who believe that others, chance, or fate control what happens in their lives, are less likely to take responsibility or hold themselves accountable because of their belief that forces outside themselves are responsible.

Increasing the importance of maintaining an elevated sense of responsibility and accountability is the apparently innate propensity for people to reject responsibility and accountability. The "victim mentality" is one example—the pervasive mind-set that "it is not my fault; I am the victim of some circumstance." The mind-set is illustrated when criminals (or their lawyers) habitually attempt to lay the blame for their crimes on society, their upbringing, racism, socioeconomic status, mental state, etc. Another example of the mind-set can be found in college students. On graded assignments or exams, students are likely to say something like, "I made an A" and/or, "He gave me an F." Notice the different mind-set? They made the A, but were given the F. We naturally take responsibility for successes, but to preserve our self-esteem, we'll gladly become a victim to make our failures easier to handle. It's human nature.

> Most people do not really want freedom, because
> freedom involves responsibility, and most people are
> frightened of responsibility.
> —Sigmund Freud, Austrian neurologist and founding.
> father of psychoanalysis

Responsibility and accountability mean no excuses, ever—leaders of character do not make excuses or accept excuses from themselves or others, because an excuse can be found for anything and everything that goes wrong. Excuses are little more than a way for us to let ourselves off the hook or lower standards and expectations. Excuses also have an eerie way of becoming self-fulfilling prophecies. In other words, if we think we're going to fail, we're right; we will because we can find an excuse for any failure.

No excuses—nothing of any value will ever come from an excuse—nothing!

> An excuse is worse and more terrible than a lie, for an
> excuse is a lie guarded.
> —Pope John Paul II, pope and leader of the Catholic
> Church

Responsibility and accountability also mean no blaming, ever. In fact, one universally accepted leadership truth is the leader always takes minimal credit for successes and maximum blame for failures because a leader is supposed to build up followers. Blaming and excuses are really the same thing; blame is simply an excuse aimed at someone or something else. Like the college student example, it is easier to lay the blame on the teacher for a poor grade than it is to look in the mirror at our own faults, weaknesses, or failures.

> A man can fail many times, but he isn't a failure until
> he begins to blame somebody else.
> —John Burroughs, American naturalist and essayist

To combat this natural propensity, responsible leaders work to develop a strong internal locus of control and accept all life events as learning experiences—both good and bad events. They consciously use bad learning experiences as motivation to make changes to their own life. If caught up in an accident, even if someone else is at fault, responsible leaders accept it as a lesson to be more watchful and change the way they do things.

Responsibility is the work of leadership, and accountability is the price of leadership. Showing others how to be more responsible and accountable may be some of the most important duties of a leader. No doubt society could certainly benefit from much more responsibility and accountability.

A responsible and accountable leader is the leader the world needs out front leading.

CHAPTER 41

Sacrifice

Sacrifice means giving up something of value for the benefit of someone else. It means putting other people's wants and needs ahead of our own. For leaders, it means giving of ourselves—our time, energy, and other resources and assets—to benefit others. Sacrifice is inherent in character-based leadership because leaders of character do not lead for their own benefit or ego, but instead, they lead to be of service to others.

Servant leadership is a concept often cited in leadership that directly correlates with sacrifice. Servant leadership suggests that the leader acts as a servant to followers, the leader is the servant of his or her followers, or the leader sacrifices himself or herself for others. The servant leadership concept, while a virtuous and grand idea, is perhaps more of a great management style than a leadership style or concept simply because leaders are servants by default. Servitude is part of the leadership job description, especially with character-based leadership. However, it is an extremely beneficial and even novel idea in the area of management—the manager as servant to his or her subordinates. What a great way to make subordinates feel important and empowered.

To be a leader is to be a servant—to be a leader is to sacrifice.

One way to gain a better appreciation and understanding of sacrifice is to study the lives and stories of some of the world-changing leaders whose lives and leadership were almost completely defined by their sacrifice. Great leaders like Mahatma Gandhi, Mother Teresa, Abraham Lincoln, Nelson Mandela, Martin Luther King Jr., and Winston Churchill spent much of their lives sacrificing and serving others. Some sacrificed their very life. While we might not have to sacrifice as much as they did, all of us can certainly be better at giving of ourselves.

The world would be a different place if the people in the list above had not done what they did, but those of us in America have another great everyday example of sacrifice: our military personnel. American military personnel sacrifice immensely by putting their lives on the line to protect not only the country's freedom and way of life, but also the lives of people in countless other countries, some that even hate America. There's no place on earth and no other civilization since the dawn of time like America, and the country owes a large part of its greatness to the US military because the old saying is absolutely true: "Freedom is not free." Like soldiers, when we decide to become leaders, we know up front that we are going to be giving up something, we are going to sacrifice—there is a price to pay to be a leader.

> Sacrifice is a part of life. It's supposed to be. It's not
> something to regret. It's something to aspire to.
> —Mitch Albom, author, journalist, screenwriter,
> dramatist, and musician

Sacrifice is a conscious choice—a noble choice—that all leaders make.

Sacrifice is not just all about giving up something; leaders benefit from sacrificing through *the power of reciprocity.* The power of reciprocity submits that what you give is what you get back; what goes around comes around; or whatever it is you want, give it first and it will come back to you. The power of reciprocity assures that if we sacrifice for others, we will be repaid. We have a natural humanistic need to be square with others (well, most of us). When someone does something that makes us feel like we owe them—that guttural urge deep inside makes us want to pay them back.

What makes the concept of reciprocity so strong is the deep and potent human emotion of gratitude. Gratitude is such a strong emotion because when someone makes our life better, we are innately geared to feel obligated to return the deed. As extremely social beings, if someone helps our survival or success, we are bound by a force deep inside us to repay them.

> Gratitude is not only the greatest of virtues, but the parent of all the others.
> —Marcus Tullius Cicero, Roman philosopher, statesman, lawyer, and orator

Perhaps one of the most important factors in sacrifice is in the good, fulfilling, and positive feelings we get from helping others. Anyone who participates in community service knows the feeling well. There is little as uplifting as helping those who may be less fortunate. Furthermore, anyone who has ever secretly helped someone without them or anyone else ever knowing about it knows the incredibly warm sense of satisfaction that comes from it. The warm sense of satisfaction is a leader's payment.

> It is one of the most beautiful compensations of life
> that no man can sincerely try to help another without
> helping himself.
> —Ralph Waldo Emerson, American essayist, lecturer,
> and poet

> The sacrifice which causes sorrow to the doer of the
> sacrifice is no sacrifice. Real sacrifice lightens the
> mind of the doer and gives him a sense of peace and
> joy. The Buddha gave up the pleasures of life because
> they had become painful to him.
> —Mohandas Mahatma Gandhi, the preeminent
> leader of nationalism in British-ruled India

An important point must be clear: sacrificing does not mean throwing away our personal lives—far from it. In fact, just like compassion, too much sacrifice is detrimental or deadly, so it must be measured. Sacrificing too much of ourselves will result in us losing everything. A leader's own personal prosperity and success must be a priority because ambition for personal success also motivates us to be better leaders and givers. Ambition is a beneficial desire because the more successful we are in life, the healthier all aspects of our life are, including our leadership. Our ambition must be for as great an overall life as possible, but never at the expense of others. Leaders believe in the philosophy that "all boats rise with the tide," the more we are able to achieve, the more we are able to give back in a virtuous cycle.

Great achievement is usually born of great sacrifice,
and is never the result of selfishness.
—Napoleon Hill, personal success author

Great leaders sacrifice greatly.

CHAPTER 42

Sense of Humor

Sense of humor is a person's ability to find and appreciate humor or comedy in funny or even ordinary everyday situations—it is the disposition of someone who is inclined to find amusement, humor, and fun in most everything they do. A person with a good sense of humor is able to laugh at and enjoy many situations that others do not necessarily find funny or fun.

> Sometimes, a sense of humor is critical in
> leadership—things cannot be serious all the time,
> we've got to have fun and enjoy what we're doing or
> we're doing the wrong thing.
> —Lt. General William T. Lord, USAF (retired)

> A sense of humor is part of the art of leadership, of
> getting along with people, of getting things done.
> —Dwight D. Eisenhower, thirty-fourth president of
> the United States

A sense of humor might seem an odd attribute for a leader of character, but humor is an extraordinarily powerful universal social harmonizer; handy in just about every situation. Most situations, even serious situations, benefit from a little levity, and most everyone enjoys humor and having fun sometimes. Truth is, if followers don't have some fun, they are not likely to follow for long because humor attracts people, lack of humor does not. People without a sense of humor will generally come off as unfriendly, stoic, stuffy, or just plain unlikable because we naturally equate likability with happiness, laughter, smiling, and fun. Fun and humor can make the worst situations a lot better; that is a leader's job, to make situations better.

As a matter of fact, it would be difficult for any successful leader to not have a sense of humor because of the importance of a positive upbeat attitude along with a healthy optimism. A great sense of humor certainly promotes and supports a positive attitude as well as a positive outlook (optimism).

A sense of humor proves a leader is human—and it improves our humanity.

Following are some great quotes that illustrate the importance of a sense of humor:

> A sense of humor … is needed armor. Joy in one's heart and some laughter on one's lips is a sign that the person down deep has a pretty good grasp of life.
> —Hugh Sidey, American journalist for *Life* and *Time* magazines

> If you could choose one characteristic that would get you through life, choose a sense of humor.
> —Jennifer Jones, Academy Award-winning actress

No mind is thoroughly well organized that is deficient in a sense of humor.
—Samuel Taylor Coleridge, English poet, critic, and philosopher

The more seriously you take yourself, the less seriously everyone else will take you.

CHAPTER 43

Trustworthiness

Trustworthiness is the level or measure of how much others can believe, believe in, depend upon, or rely upon you. Being trustworthy means a person is honest, dependable, and reliable, and can be trusted to be honorable, moral, and ethical. Trustworthiness is the level of trust and confidence followers have in the leader. Being trusted is a leader's most critical requirement—especially leaders of character.

> To be trusted is a greater compliment than to be loved.
> —George MacDonald, Scottish author, poet, and minister

Great leaders measure their leadership potency and success in trustworthiness.

The main reason trust is so incredibly important to leaders is it is the cornerstone of every human relationship; the very thing leadership is about. Trust is the lifeblood of all of our relationships in every role we play throughout our entire life, especially those closest to us (e.g., family, friends, etc.). For leaders, our trustworthiness is important to everyone we influence and everyone we might influence, including people we do not even know personally. Pro athletes and celebrities, politicians, and high-level leaders in organizations influence many people they will never actually meet and their trustworthiness is paramount to them as well.

The fact about trustworthiness that leaders must always be meticulously aware of is if trust is sacrificed in a relationship—any relationship—if the relationship survives at all, the trust will be forever diminished and will *never* be fully regained. Some might say this is not true, that we must always forgive those we love; however, we humans might be able to forgive, but we never forget when our trust is betrayed. Besides, we are only capable of forgiving up to a certain point; there is some level of trust destruction that will destroy any relationship. Regardless of the relationship, leaders must always be concerned that even the slightest damage to trust will have lasting effects, so trustworthiness must be guarded at all costs.

> Trust is like a mirror—once it's broken, it's never seen
> the same again and no matter how hard you try to put
> it back together, the cracks will always show.
> —Unknown

Trust is so precious and sacred that if sacrificed or damaged, it is forever scarred and diminished; its original luster never to be returned.

Making matters worse, trust is also fairly fragile and elusive. A very true old saying states that "it can take years to build trust, but it can be destroyed in a moment" with just one wrong word or action. Over the years, several politicians and celebrities have lost their jobs or positions and their credibility and trustworthiness because of a single stupid, mean, or absolutely wrong statement. A single sentence has significantly damaged many people's lives, because trust is that fragile. Salespeople, who are especially attuned to this issue, sometimes spend years developing trusting relationships with prospects or clients, all the while knowing one wrong move or word, one lie or untruth, or one broken promise can bring it all crashing down. This delicate nature of trust is one of the main reasons it is so preciously valuable.

> Trust is like the air we breathe. When it's present,
> nobody really notices. But when it's absent, everybody
> notices.
> —Warren Buffet, American business magnate,
> investor, and philanthropist

Fittingly, trust is also the cornerstone of leadership and influence because a leader will only influence those who trust him or her. In fact, trust is a prerequisite to leadership; it must already be in place before a leader can even take the lead. People will not even associate with anyone they do not trust in the first place.

> The glue that holds all relationships together—
> including the relationship between the leader and the
> led—is trust, and trust is based on integrity.
> —Brian Tracy, self-help author and motivational
> speaker

While Brian Tracy's quote got the glue part right, trust is based on many more elements than just integrity. Trustworthiness is directly based on, and developed by, being authentic, committed, competent, confident, courageous, credible, honest, honorable, humble, moral, optimistic, persistent, professional, respectful, responsible, and accountable, in addition to maintaining integrity. There are few aspects of our leadership and our lives that trust does not impact.

The true wealth of a leader is measured in trustworthiness.

Following are some specific actions based on the elements that will develop trustworthiness:

- Highly value and cherish all relationships.
- Fiercely maintain honesty and honor.
- Communicate—often, clearly, truthfully, and completely.
- Do what you say you're going to do, be reliable, always keep your word.
- Make your values public, and openly and boldly live by them every day.
- Readily admit when you're wrong—accept blame, even if it is not yours.
- Never lash out in anger (more damage is done by words than bombs).
- Trust; people have a way of living up to, or down to, expectations.
- Be aware of, and publically acknowledge, your weaknesses.
- Passionately maintain morality.
- Always show compassion for others.

- Make sure every day, and in every situation, your behavior, actions, and activities align with your honor, morals, and values.

> The only way to make a man trustworthy is to trust him.
> —Henry Lewis Stimson, American statesman, lawyer, and politician

Trust is vital to relationships, but it also has value in other contexts. Because of the monumental costs that have been incurred by businesses, organizations, and even government over the last several years due completely to unethical behaviors, the value of trust has been a major topic of study and discussion by many researchers and thinkers. There have now been many studies that valuated trust in organizations and businesses, so trust's worth has now been well documented.

All other factors accounted for, companies with a trustworthy reputation are much more profitable and develop a significantly higher market value in a much shorter time period than similar companies with not-so-trustworthy reputations. Also, the stock prices of trustworthy companies maintain a higher value over time, and innovation and productivity are much higher in trustworthy organizations as well. And of course, as consumers, most of us consciously know that we will only do business or interact with organizations that we trust. All of this just supports the importance and value of trust to everyone.

Leadership and influence only exist where trust exists. They are always proportional.

CHAPTER 44

Values

Values are ideals, principles, standards, and beliefs held deeply important by a person or group. Values are not physical things or goals like family, money, or success; instead, they are generally ideals or ideologies, strong beliefs, or principles usually based on moral character components like honor, morality, and other virtues. Values are the genuinely personal beliefs, standards, and judgments about what we truly believe to be the most valuable and important principles to follow and uphold in our lives.

Values are a major topic in leadership books and discussions, so several variations on the concept have been introduced over time that should be clarified.

Personal values are what have been described above; these are our own individual values.

Core values simply refer to our most centrally important values—the most essential, or "core" of our values. *Core values* and *values* are often used synonymously because the word *value* has numerous dictionary definitions and it is used in several different contexts; therefore, adding the word *core* helps designate that it is referring specifically to the context of leaders.

Shared core values, or shared values, have to do with groups, or organizations, of people who are bound together by common personal values that each individual holds. Organizational shared core values are the principles and ideals that guide an organization's culture, conduct, and interactions with the external world. Because shared core values are also the personal values of the members of the group, groups generally attract other people with similar personal values, creating an ingrained long-term or perpetual shared-value culture. Anyone entering such a group who does not share the group's obvious defined values will generally be pushed out from their own discomfort from nonaligned values.

Values may seem like too lofty and abstract an idea to be of much consequence, but this is one of the most critical of all of the elements for everyone because our values are what determine or drive every decision we make, especially major life decisions. For example, if self-sufficiency is one of our deeply held values, throughout our lives we will make decisions and choices, even subconsciously, to follow education or career paths that we expect will lead toward independence. If character is one of our values, we will make decisions that support or develop our character, and strive to not make decisions that might negatively impact our character. Of course if our values are not so virtuous, our decisions and choices will lead our life in that direction as well.

Because our values have such an impact on our entire life, and the lives of those we go through life with, intimately knowing our values may be the most important self-knowledge we can acquire. Not being fully aware of our values can (or will) result in us going through life randomly, accomplishing little, not ever really heading or getting anywhere, and never feeling satisfied or fulfilled. Being acutely aware of our values even makes living life simpler because many of the major decisions in life will literally make themselves when a choice obviously aligns with our values. Anyone with considerable life experience can reflect back on past major decisions and likely discover the values they held at the time that guided the decision they made. Some of us can look back at regretful decisions and we are likely to see that we chose a path that did not align with our values.

The question now is, How do we determine what our own values are? To discover our values, we have to learn to listen intently to our conscience and our inner voice to honestly determine the answer to the following questions: What do I stand for? What do I really believe in? What would I vehemently defend? What does my conscience say? What surges my emotions? What makes me jump out of bed in the morning? What keeps me awake at night? What am I truly passionate about? What do I truly, honestly care about?

One method to assist in finding your values can be found in the appendix of this book. The method includes a list of over three hundred prospective values (the list is certainly not complete; there are many more potential values that can be added to the list). The process is to simply scan the list, choosing and marking words that resonate with you, touch you, or scream at you. It is likely that on some words your heart and mind will tell you immediately that it is important to you. Most importantly, you must be brutally honest with yourself and not choose values or words just because you think that is what others expect you to value; choose those that you know you value. When you come to the end of the list, go back through and pick your top ten or so of those you have already chosen. Being forced to choose your top-priority values will force you to further clarify and refine your thoughts and feelings about what you truly value. The exercise will at least compel you to begin consciously taking stock of what you hold to be important. Over time your values will become clearer and clearer to you if you continue the process on a regular basis.

One question often asked is, Are values static; do they change? They do change; values evolve. Just like character, personal values are not permanent and change throughout our life. As we grow older and pass from chapter to chapter in our lives, new values arise and less beneficial values fade. In fact, throughout our life, as our responsibilities and roles change, we will become increasingly aware of principles and values that we should be more attuned to, and some we should be less attuned to as well.

The tough question is, What if we find that what we are doing does not align with our values? Or, what do we do when we realize we are part of a group or organization that does not share our values? Truthfully, these kinds of mismatches naturally fix themselves eventually because the negativity of a values mismatch situation will naturally repel us, while the positive feelings of a potential match attract us away from the mismatch. We also have to accept that we may sometimes be stuck for some time in a values mismatch situation, especially in the case of a job, but we can never let the situation dictate our values. To be the happiest, most effective, and most successful, the best alternative is to find or build groups or organizations with clear values that align with our own personal values.

Our values are our internal compass; they point us toward our true personal north or best direction. If we pay attention, our values will lead us in the right direction.

In order to further clarify the concept of values, following are some examples of organizational or group core value statements. The benefit of these values statements is to offer real-world examples that might ring important to each of us in attempting to define our own personal values.

Leaders of Character Core Values:

- **Character:** above all else
- **Leadership:** stepping up to lead when someone needs to step up
- **Professionalism:** elevated standards of behavior and achievement
- **Legacy:** development of the next generation of leaders and pursuit of an enduring impact on the world

---

Zappos Family Core Values[12]: "As we grow as a company, it has become more and more important to explicitly define the core values from which we develop our culture, our brand, and our business strategies. These are the ten core values that we live by:

---

[12] Zappos Family Core Values. http://about.zappos.com/our-unique-culture/zappos-core-values. Web. 19 June 2013

1. Deliver WOW through Service
2. Embrace and Drive Change
3. Create Fun and a Little Weirdness
4. Be Adventurous, Creative, and Open-Minded
5. Pursue Growth and Learning
6. Build Open and Honest Relationships with Communication
7. Build a Positive Team and Family Spirit
8. Do More with Less
9. Be Passionate and Determined
10. Be Humble"

Though lengthy, the following values statements are inserted in their entirety because they are very thorough, comprehensive, and we can learn so much from them. Countless hours (decades or centuries probably), thought, passion, energy, blood, and lives went into the foundation of these statements. There could be little area in an airman's life that is not guided by these statements, nor could there be a better guide for us to follow in developing our own values.

The United States Air Force Core Values[13] are "Integrity first; Service before self; and Excellence in all we do." Following is an explanation of these values taken from their website:

---

[13] About the Air Force: Our Values. http://www.airforce.com/learn-about/our-values/. Web. 19 June 2013

Our Values

Whoever you are and wherever you fit on the Air Force team, the Core Values are what you will live by and learn to cherish.

The Core Values are much more than minimum standards. They remind us what it takes to get the mission done. They inspire us to do our very best at all times. They are the common bond among all comrades in arms, and they are the glue that unifies the Force and ties us to the great warriors and public servants of the past.

The First Core Value: Integrity First

The Airman is a person of integrity, courage, and conviction.

Integrity is a character trait. It is the willingness to do what is right even when no one is looking. It is the moral compass, the inner voice, the voice of self-control, and the basis for the trust imperative in today's military.

Integrity is the ability to hold together and properly regulate all of the elements of a personality. A person of integrity, for example, is capable of acting on conviction. A person of integrity can control impulses and appetites.

But integrity also covers several other moral traits indispensable to national service.

Courage: A person of integrity possesses moral courage and does what is right even if the personal cost is high.

Honesty: Honesty is the hallmark of the military professional because in the military, our word must be our bond. We don't pencil-whip training reports, we don't cover up tech data violations, we don't falsify documents, and we don't write misleading operational readiness messages. The bottom line is: We don't lie, and we can't justify any deviation.

Responsibility: No person of integrity is irresponsible; a person of true integrity acknowledges his/her duties and acts accordingly.

Accountability: No person of integrity tries to shift the blame to others or take credit for the work of others. "The buck stops here" says it best.

Justice: A person of integrity practices justice. Those who do similar things must get similar rewards or similar punishments.

Openness: Professionals of integrity encourage a free flow of information within the organization. They seek feedback from all directions to ensure they are fulfilling key responsibilities, and they are never afraid to allow anyone at any time to examine how they do business.

Self-respect: To have integrity is also to respect oneself as a professional and a human being. A person of integrity does not behave in ways that would bring discredit upon himself or herself or the organization to which he or she belongs.

Humility: A person of integrity grasps and is sobered by the awesome task of defending the Constitution of the United States of America.

The Second Core Value: Service before Self

An Airman's professional duties always take precedence over personal desires.

Service before self tells us that professional duties take precedence over personal desires. At the very least, it includes the following behaviors:

Rule following: To serve is to do one's duty, and our duties are most commonly expressed through rules. While it may be the case that professionals are expected to exercise judgment in the performance of their duties, good professionals understand that rules have a reason for being—and the default position must be to follow those rules unless there is a clear, operational reason for refusing to do so.

Respect for others: Service before self tells us also that a good leader places the troops ahead of his/her personal comfort. We must always act in the certain knowledge that all persons possess a fundamental worth as human beings.

Discipline and self-control: Professionals cannot indulge themselves in self-pity, discouragement, anger, frustration, or defeatism. They have a fundamental moral obligation to the persons they lead to strike a tone of confidence and forward-looking optimism. More specifically, they are expected to exercise control in the following areas:

Anger: Military professionals and especially commanders at all echelons are expected to refrain from displays of anger that would bring discredit upon themselves and/or the Air Force.

Appetites: Those who allow their appetites to drive them to make sexual overtures to subordinates are unfit for military service. Likewise, the excessive consumption of alcohol casts doubt on an individual's fitness.

Religious toleration: Military professionals must remember that religious choice is a matter of individual conscience. Professionals—and especially commanders—must not take it upon themselves to change or coercively influence the religious views of subordinates.

The Third Core Value: Excellence in All We Do

Every American Airman strives for continual improvement in self and service.

Excellence in all we do directs us to develop a sustained passion for continuous improvement and innovation that will propel the Air Force into a long-term, upward spiral of accomplishment and performance.

Product/service excellence: We must focus on providing services and generating products that fully respond to customer wants and anticipate customer needs, and we must do so within the boundaries established by the tax-paying public.

Personal excellence: Military professionals must seek out and complete professional military education, stay in physical and mental shape, and continue to refresh their general educational backgrounds.

Community excellence: Community excellence is achieved when the members of an organization can work together to successfully reach a common goal in an atmosphere that is free from fear and that preserves individual self-worth. Some of the factors influencing interpersonal excellence are:

Mutual respect: Genuine respect involves viewing another person as an individual of fundamental worth. Obviously, this means that a person is never judged on the basis of his/her possession of an attribute that places him/her in some racial, ethnic, economic, or gender-based category.

Benefit of the doubt: Working hand in glove with mutual respect is that attitude that says all coworkers are innocent until proven guilty. Before rushing to judgment about a person or his/her behavior, it is important to have the whole story.

Resources excellence: Excellence in all we do also demands that we aggressively implement policies to ensure the best possible cradle-to-grave management of resources.

Material resources excellence: Military professionals have an obligation to ensure that all of the equipment and property they ask for is mission essential. This means that residual funds at the end of the year should not be used to purchase "nice to have" add-ons.

Human resources excellence: Human resources excellence means that we recruit, train, promote, and retain those who can do the best job for us.

Operations excellence: There are two kinds of operations excellence: internal and external.

Excellence of internal operations: This form of excellence pertains to the way we do business internal to the Air Force from the unit level to Air Force Headquarters. It involves respect on the unit level and a total commitment to maximizing the Air Force team effort.

Excellence of external operations: This form of excellence pertains to the way in which we treat the world around us as we conduct our operations. In peacetime, for example, we must be sensitive to the rules governing environmental pollution, and in wartime we are required to obey the laws of war.

———

Of equal prominence, significance, and expanse, following are the complete United States Army Core Values[14] taken from their website.

The Army Values

Many people know what the words Loyalty, Duty, Respect, Selfless Service, Honor, Integrity, and Personal Courage mean. But how often do you see someone actually live up to them? Soldiers learn these values in detail during Basic Combat Training (BCT), from then on they live them every day in everything they do—whether they're on the job or off. In short, the Seven Core Army Values listed below are what being a Soldier is all about.

---

[14] Army Values. http://www.army.mil/values/index.html. © 2013 U.S. Army. Web. 19 June 2013

Loyalty

Bear true faith and allegiance to the US Constitution, the Army, your unit, and other Soldiers. Bearing true faith and allegiance is a matter of believing in and devoting yourself to something or someone. A loyal Soldier is one who supports the leadership and stands up for fellow Soldiers. By wearing the uniform of the US Army you are expressing your loyalty. And by doing your share, you show your loyalty to your unit.

Duty

Fulfill your obligations. Doing your duty means more than carrying out your assigned tasks. Duty means being able to accomplish tasks as part of a team. The work of the US Army is a complex combination of missions, tasks, and responsibilities—all in constant motion. Our work entails building one assignment onto another. You fulfill your obligations as a part of your unit every time you resist the temptation to take "shortcuts" that might undermine the integrity of the final product.

Respect

Treat people as they should be treated. In the Soldier's Code, we pledge to "treat others with dignity and respect while expecting others to do the same." Respect is what allows us to appreciate the best in other people. Respect is trusting that all people have done their jobs and fulfilled their duty. And self-respect is a vital ingredient with the Army value of respect, which results from knowing you have put forth your best effort. The Army is one team and each of us has something to contribute.

Selfless Service

Put the welfare of the nation, the Army, and your subordinates before your own. Selfless service is larger than just one person. In serving your country, you are doing your duty loyally without thought of recognition or gain. The basic building block of selfless service is the commitment of each team member to go a little further, endure a little longer, and look a little closer to see how he or she can add to the effort.

Honor

Live up to Army values. The nation's highest military award is The Medal of Honor. This award goes to Soldiers who make honor a matter of daily living—Soldiers who develop the habit of being honorable, and solidify that habit with every value choice they make. Honor is a matter of carrying out, acting, and living the values of respect, duty, loyalty, selfless service, integrity, and personal courage in everything you do.

Integrity

Do what's right, legally and morally. Integrity is a quality you develop by adhering to moral principles. It requires that you do and say nothing that deceives others. As your integrity grows, so does the trust others place in you. The more choices you make based on integrity, the more this highly prized value will affect your relationships with family and friends, and, finally, the fundamental acceptance of yourself.

Personal Courage

Face fear, danger, or adversity (physical or moral). Personal courage has long been associated with our Army. With physical courage, it is a matter of enduring physical duress and at times risking personal safety. Facing moral fear or adversity may be a long, slow process of continuing forward on the right path, especially if taking those actions is not popular with others. You can build your personal courage by daily standing up for and acting upon the things that you know are honorable.

And in equal significance, following are the United States Navy and Marines Core Values[15] taken from their website.

The United States Navy

Throughout its history, the Navy has successfully met all its challenges. America's naval service began during the American Revolution, when on Oct. 13, 1775, the Continental Congress authorized a few small ships, creating the Continental Navy. Esek Hopkins was appointed commander in chief and 22 officers were commissioned, including John Paul Jones.

From those early days of naval service, certain bedrock principles or core values have carried on to today. They consist of three basic principles.

---

[15] The U.S. Navy. http://www.navy.mil/navydata/nav_legacy.asp?id=193. Web. 19 June 2013

Honor: "I will bear true faith and allegiance ..." Accordingly, we will: Conduct ourselves in the highest ethical manner in all relationships with peers, superiors, and subordinates; Be honest and truthful in our dealings with each other, and with those outside the Navy; Be willing to make honest recommendations and accept those of junior personnel; Encourage new ideas and deliver the bad news, even when it is unpopular; Abide by an uncompromising code of integrity, taking responsibility for our actions and keeping our word; Fulfill or exceed our legal and ethical responsibilities in our public and personal lives twenty-four hours a day. Illegal or improper behavior or even the appearance of such behavior will not be tolerated. We are accountable for our professional and personal behavior. We will be mindful of the privilege to serve our fellow Americans.

Courage: "I will support and defend ..." Accordingly, we will have: Courage to meet the demands of our profession and the mission when it is hazardous, demanding, or otherwise difficult; Make decisions in the best interest of the Navy and the nation, without regard to personal consequences; Meet these challenges while adhering to a higher standard of personal conduct and decency; Be loyal to our nation, ensuring the resources entrusted to us are used in an honest, careful, and efficient way. Courage is the value that gives us the moral and mental strength to do what is right, even in the face of personal or professional adversity.

Commitment: "I will obey the orders ..." Accordingly, we will: Demand respect up and down the chain of command; Care for the safety, professional, personal, and spiritual well-being of our people; Show respect toward all people without regard to race, religion, or gender; Treat each individual with human dignity; Be committed to positive change and constant improvement; Exhibit the highest degree of moral character, technical excellence, quality, and competence in what we have been trained to do. The day-to-day duty of every Navy man and woman is to work together as a team to improve the quality of our work, our people, and ourselves.

These are the CORE VALUES of the United States Navy.

Shared core values are a critical factor in the strength, prosperity, and continuity of all organizations and groups.

CHAPTER 45

Vision

Vision is a person's ability to create and picture a mental image of a potential future, result, or outcome in their mind or imagination. Vision is an idea, image, picture, or concept formed by our imagination. For leaders, vision is the expected or hoped for results of our influence; the impact or results we want to have as leaders. If we are leading, something is happening and some kind of change is taking place, and it is the leader's responsibility to have an idea, a vision, of where the change should go. The leader's responsibility is to guide change toward an envisioned goal or result—a vision.

The vision is the point in the future where the leader wants to take others.

The following quote illustrates the absolute importance of vision to leaders.

> Vision is everything for a leader. It is utterly
> indispensable. Why? Because vision leads the leader.
> It paints the target. It sparks and fuels the fire within,
> and draws him forward. It is also the fire lighter

for others who follow that leader. Show me a leader without vision, and I'll show you someone who isn't going anywhere. At best, he is traveling in circles.

—John Maxwell, leadership author, teacher, speaker, and guru

A leader must lead towards a specific envisioned goal or else the direction, and the change, will be random, haphazard, and of no progress or advancement at all.

Vision is the element that primarily sets leaders apart; it is part of the true essence or foundation of the act, art, or skill of leadership. While vision may seem to be some grand concept, in its most simple form it is actually just the desired outcome of a leader's influence, no matter how minor. For instance, a leader of character's intention of making the world a better place is a vision in itself (which also means a vision does not have to have an ending; it can be the results of ongoing change). If a leader always dresses and behaves above average in setting the example with the hope others will rise to the same level, the vision is others rising to the same level. If we publicly articulate and live by our values with the hope and expectation that others will follow suit, that hope and expectation is our vision.

To further clarify, following are a few examples of ordinary vision in various everyday situations:

- When entering college, the hoped for end result is a degree. That degree is the vision, and we lead ourselves toward making that vision a reality.

- When preparing to build a new home, the first step is having blueprints drawn up. Those blueprints are a technical vision of the home in the future.
- When an entrepreneur has an idea for a new business, the first thing she does is write a business plan. The business plan is the vision of what she wants the business to look like someday. Clarifying the vision through the process of drafting the plan is the real value of the project.
- In the 1940s, a man took his daughters to an amusement park in California. The park was run-down, unkempt, and dirty. The condition of the park infuriated him and in his disgust he had a vision that there should be a place for families to go where everyone in the family could enjoy themselves. That vision was refined and clarified into Disneyland. The man was Walt Disney.

The question might be asked, Can the skill of creating a viable vision be learned or developed? All visions are intentionally and consciously created, developed, refined, clarified, and communicated. Of course, lots of knowledge of the specific situation and some imagination and creativity are required. However, every leader does not necessarily have to create the vision; most will pursue some version of an existing vision. If leading in an organization, the ultimate goal of the organization will guide or define the vision. Truthfully, everyone in most organizations is ultimately following the vision of the founder (which also illustrates the phenomenal power of vision). For instance, everyone in Disney today is pursuing Walt Disney's vision that he developed in the early 1950s. Mr. Disney's vision is still guiding the company decades after the man himself passed away.

Walt Disney's vision brings up a related skill: imagination. Imagination is what is used to create vision, but it is also very valuable in other ways. For instance it has been proven that "mental practice" or just thinking through the motions or details of an activity is almost the same as doing it for real to our subconscious mind. All great athletes know the power of such mental practice. Professional archers talk of visualizing arrows hitting the bull's-eye every waking moment (and even in their dreams) before a big tournament. Basketball players also practice the same, visualizing the ball going in the basket over and over. This practice can be effective with everyday activities as well. Mental practice lets our mind's eye see success again and again so that in real time our conscious mind, which is impacted by every distraction, can be minimized in the activity by our well-practiced subconscious. If imagination is such a powerful tool for Walt Disney and pro athletes, then it is certainly a skill leaders should develop as well.

To be successful, a vision must be practical, realistic, and reachable. Practical because people want what they do to make sense and be beneficial to themselves and others. Realistic and reachable because people will not even try to reach a goal or vision if they feel it is unrealistic or unreachable. People do not like to waste their time or fail, so a vision that is impractical, unrealistic, or unreachable is no more than a fairy tale—albeit usually without a happy ending. A vision is also worthless if no one else knows about it, if it is not communicated. The real value in a vision cannot be realized until it becomes a vision shared by other people who wish to make it a reality. Clearly and effectively communicating the vision and getting others to adopt it is one of a leader's most critical duties.

Being a great vision communicator and salesperson is a requirement to being a great leader.

One benefit of a clearly communicated vision is the motivational power a clear vision has on others. People are naturally motivated by knowing which way to go, and which direction is the right direction. A clear, shared vision is energizing because everyone is going the same direction with the same goal. There is something very stimulating and empowering to individual members when everyone in a group or organization is pulling together, working together to create something new, or striving side by side to reach the same goal or vision. It is a leader's job to tap that natural energy.

Another benefit of vision is in the influence goals have on people. Most very successful people are goal-oriented, meaning they set many successive goals to take advantage of the self-motivating power of striving to reach goals. This mind-set is a huge factor in success at anything because people can and do excel beyond their own perceived capabilities and limitations when striving to reach a goal. This quote from one of the most influential leaders in human history supports this idea:

> Glory lies in the attempt to reach one's goal and not
> in reaching it.
> —Mohandas Mahatma Gandhi, the preeminent
> leader of nationalism in British-ruled India

There is a difference between vision and goals: vision is not static or measureable, whereas goals should be both. Goals are very specific and concrete in order to steady our aim and purpose. Goals should be measureable so that progress can be benchmarked. A vision, on the other hand, is never static or concrete because it becomes clearer and more refined as it progresses toward reality. Leaders set concrete, measureable goals and leave them alone, but regularly revisit and reclarify the vision to keep it fresh, current, and viable.

> Arriving at one goal is the starting point to another.
> —John Dewey, philosopher, psychologist, and
> educational reformer

Leaders develop and communicate vision and goals—it is just what leaders do. Both are critical leadership skills. This key leadership responsibility is one of the most important and valuable duties leaders perform. Vision, or how well we develop it and clearly communicate it, will significantly determine our leadership success and legacy.

Vision is a leader's guide, third eye, pilot, and ultimate reason to lead.

CHAPTER 46

Willingness to Lead

Willingness to lead is a leader's ready inclination to step up and lead, doing all that is required whenever and wherever leadership is needed. It is a quick readiness and proclivity to eagerly perform all the tasks, duties, and responsibilities required of a leader. For leaders of character, willingness to lead means an eagerness to step up and offer character-based leadership whenever and wherever leadership is needed.

Willingness to quickly and readily step up to lead is automatic for leaders of character. The behavior becomes automatic through the passion of working on and developing all of the attributes, practices, and principles detailed in this book. Every element discussed in this book is vital in

- getting followers to accept us as a leader.
- helping us be a more impactful and successful leader.
- reducing the risk inherent in stepping up and putting ourselves on the line.
- increasing and multiplying influence.
- increasing our effectiveness and efficiency as leaders.
- increasing the amount of enjoyment we get from leading.

- improving all of our relationships.
- increasing the longevity of our leadership.
- writing our legacy.

Willingness to step up and lead when leadership is needed is in the nucleus of every cell in a leader of character's body.

Willingness to lead means a leader is also a doer. A doer is one of those rare people who just seem to get more done than anyone else. Non-doers are completely unaware that they are non-doers, they simply do not notice what should be done or needs to be done, or they sit back and wait to see if someone else will do it. Non-doers usually wait to be told exactly what they need to do, or have to do, then mechanically do just that. Doers, on the other hand, are the ones who

- are always busy, but they are also the first to jump on a new job or project anyway.
- the boss always goes to when something really has to be done quickly.
- always seem to have more to do than could possibly be done; but they get it done anyway.
- always seem to be the first person there and the last to leave.
- do not need or want to be managed; they just want to be left alone to get things done.
- are more concerned about doing the job right than staying within boundaries or rules.
- are always the ones who get the most opportunities handed to them.

Every successful person was or is a doer. Anyone who ever accomplished anything significant was a doer; they certainly did not wait on someone else to do it for them. The following quotes illustrate the importance of doers:

Action is the foundational key to all success.
—Pablo Picasso, Spanish artist

Wishing and hoping and praying are poor excuses for action.
—Dennis A. Peer, author and speaker

It is not the critic who counts: not the man who points out how the strong man stumbles or where the *doer* of deeds could have done better. The credit belongs to the man who is actually in the arena, whose face is marred by dust and sweat and blood, who strives valiantly, who errs and comes up short again and again, because there is no effort without error or shortcoming, but who knows the great enthusiasms, the great devotions, who spends himself for a worthy cause; who, at the best, knows, in the end, the triumph of high achievement, and who, at the worst, if he fails, at least he fails while daring greatly, so that his place shall never be with those cold and timid souls who knew neither victory nor defeat.
—Theodore Roosevelt, twenty-sixth president of the United States

> Whenever you are asked if you can do a job, tell 'em,
> "Certainly I can!" Then get busy and find out how to
> do it.
> —Theodore Roosevelt, twenty-sixth president of the
> United States

It is imperative that the leader be a doer because the other doers—the most important people in any group or organization—will have a difficult time respecting or following a leader who is not a doer. That does not mean the leader has to do the same job or work the same way as other doers, but the leader has to be seen as a doer in his or her role.

Leaders do something! Anything! Even the wrong thing is better than doing nothing at all. With the wrong thing, at least we learn what not to do.

Included in the willingness to lead is the major duty of leaders to develop other leaders. In fact, great leaders are always on the lookout for future leaders, and even their replacements. Creating other leaders is one of a leader's highest duties because the world always has, and always will, need many more leaders. Developing a replacement long before a replacement might be needed is essential to assure the continuity of the group or organization because very few leaders have the ability to maintain exaggerated effectiveness for very long periods of time. In fact, one of the worst leadership failures is for a leader to depart without a well-developed replacement. Organizations with great leader development programs are the strongest and most enduring organizations because vibrant people and organizations need change, including leaders.

A deep-rooted willingness to lead and perform all that a leader must while being a person of strong positive virtuous character is the greatest gift a leader can give to the world.

CHAPTER 47

And Many More Elements

While the number of elements and the amount of detail covered in this book may seem considerable, everything in this book is likely just a drop in the bucket, or a scratch on the surface, of the overall science of leaders and leadership. The old saying certainly fits here: "We don't know what we don't know," so there could be enormous amounts of data, information, and details that have yet to even be illuminated in this evolving discipline. Certainly, new words and concepts will be required in order to accurately describe and define many new components and concepts.

However, no apologies or shortcuts can be made for the abstractness, complexity, or quantity of the elements; the attributes, practices, and principles of leaders of character are simply that abstract, complex, and numerous—there is no short-cut. To illustrate the point, character makes a good clarifying parallel comparison to the complexity of leadership. The incredible abstractness, complexity, numerous influencers, and number of components that form our character is infinite—likely without bounds or ends—and the same is true of leadership. Further complicating it is the fact that every leadership scenario, leader, and leader's situation is unique, fluid, and impacted by countless factors always in play. We will never discover everything that comprises our character, nor are we likely to discover every attribute, practice, and principle of leaders of character either.

However, it is quite safe to accept that the elements offered in this book entail a significant portion of any leader of character's attributes, practices, and principles, so at minimum, these elements are a great foundational starting point. It is every leader's lifetime responsibility to be cognizant of the elements that impact each of us and our personal leadership situation, and then work tirelessly to develop ourselves in every pertinent area.

SECTION 3

Additional Practices of Leaders of Character

There are a few additional important aspects that need to be pointed out about leaders of character that are not elements, but more like practices or strategies that those leaders utilize. These strategies are common or best practices. Best practices simply mean these are strategies that work. These are valuable because, while we do learn from others' mistakes, we can also learn from other's successes.

CHAPTER 48

Character-Based Decision Making

Leaders are required to make decisions and choices, that is part of the job, and a leader's decisions and choices can heavily impact other people or have significant consequences on our own lives and leadership. Decisions of such magnitude cannot be made haphazardly, but must be managed professionally; therefore, leaders develop decision-making expertise as a common facet of their leadership development. Decision making is part art and part science, very situational (just like leadership), and there is no perfect cookie-cutter formula for making the right decisions all the time in every situation. There are, however, some techniques that aid in making character-based decisions.

Several years ago a fad raced across the country with incredible speed. It was transported by the simplicity of the message and the mass production of countless bracelets transcribed with the four-letter acronym "WWJD." What Would Jesus Do? WWJD was in fact an ethical decision-making tool that young people found especially easy to use in the decisions they made in their everyday lives. When faced with a decision, especially of a potentially ethical issue, the WWJD tool would easily tell them how to make a good moral decision. This tool is still very valid for all to use.

Leaders can ask themselves, "What Would a Leader of Character Do?" (WWLCD) when faced with a tough decision, or simply ask themselves, Will this decision increase, decrease, or have no effect on my own self-view, and other people's view, of my reputation and standing as a leader of character? To be more precise, self-questioning can drill down to a specific element such as, How will this decision impact my honor?—respect?—trustworthiness?—integrity?—competence?—credibility?—and even character? Decisions of any magnitude will have one of three net impacts on the elements: positive, negative, or neither. Leaders of character always try for a *positive* impact first, then a *neither positive or negative* impact if positive is not possible. A *negative* impact is never acceptable.

Following are some examples of other questions that can be used in character-based decision making:

- If my entire family were standing here with me, what would the decision be?
- If a transcript of the entire decision, private conversations and all, was printed on the front page of the paper, would I and my family and friends be proud of my decision?
- If making this decision was being filmed for television, would I and my family and friends be proud of my decision?
- Is there any chance that I will feel guilty about this decision in the future?

While most everyday decisions in life will have no positive or negative impact on our leadership, everyone will face many decisions and choices in time that will. Our best defense is to be as prepared as possible and use whatever tool or method that works for each of us to protect our leadership and our character. The benefit in using these strategies is that our character will always be maintained, even if we make the wrong decision. The resulting clear conscience is a very valuable result.

> There is no pillow as soft as a clear conscience.
> —John Wooden, ten-time national championship
> basketball coach

CHAPTER 49

Respect of Power

The common definition of *power* is, "the capacity to exert *influence* over others." Since our definition of leadership is influence, then power and leadership are inextricably connected, so leaders of character are forced to acknowledge, monitor, respect, and even fear power.

One important distinction to note: the capacity to exert influence does not include the right to exert it. The right to exert it is authority, which is not leadership at all. People with authority are not necessarily leaders, and leaders do not necessarily have any authority. However, if we influence someone to do something, anything at all, we are exerting some kind of power, so leadership is about power as well.

History (and current news) is fraught with examples of the dangers of power and the damage, death, and destruction caused by power and the struggle for it. Everyone knows the old saying and quote from nineteenth-century English historian and writer Lord Dalberg-Acton: "*Power corrupts, but absolute power corrupts absolutely.*" "Power corrupts" simply means that power changes good people into bad people. And, absolute power changes a good person into an absolutely bad person.

There are few absolutes with people, but there is one absolute when it comes to power: no human must ever have absolute power, no matter who they are, what their intentions are, or how good a person they might be. No human is perfect or immune to the dangers of power—nobody—everybody is susceptible to corruption from too much power. History and current news repeatedly prove this absolute fact. Power, especially absolute power, leads to the desire to gain more power, and absolute power always results in the primary goal of maintaining a hold on power. The desire to maintain power always has a negative and sometimes horrific outcome.

The framers of the American Constitution knew the dangers of absolute power, learned from a long history of tyrannical monarchy and dictatorial governments, so they designed the Constitution, the electoral system, and the laws of the land to combat the dangers of anyone gaining absolute power. Power is both an important and dangerous component of leadership, but leaders, especially very influential leaders, are in a continuous battle to maintain self-control to keep power and the pursuit of more of it from controlling them. The more influence leaders gain, the more power they have and the more danger they are in of falling victim to that power.

So how do we combat the destructive force of power? One way is to be completely aware of the dangers of it. Having knowledge and an awareness of it will help us control it and give us the ability to use it in beneficial ways. Perhaps the strongest antidote to the poison of power is to value our character, integrity, honor, and values as much as anything on earth. The most important point to remember is leaders, especially leaders of character, have an absolute responsibility to use power to do good, positive, and virtuous things.

Leaders of character must balance on the precipice of power protected from its corruption and doom only by character and all of the elements.

CHAPTER 50

Self-Improvement

The only thing that is automatic in life is change and death; improvement or growth is only through intention.

Leaders of character are resolute lifetime learners, and as such, they are also resolved to continuous lifetime self-improvement. Lifetime learning, continuous development of knowledge, is one component of self-improvement, but self-improvement also covers every aspect and facet of our entire being including our physical, mental, emotional, and spiritual fitness and health. There is no part of us that does not need our conscious attention to improvement.

> You are your greatest asset. Put your time, effort and money into training, grooming, and encouraging your greatest asset.
> —Tom Hopkins, author, speaker, and sales trainer

> Every man has in himself a continent of undiscovered character. Happy is he who acts as the Columbus to his own soul.
> —Sir J. Stephen, British undersecretary of state for the American colonies

While this is a leadership book, or specifically a leader of character development book, in essence, it is as much about self-improvement as anything. Since the primary goal of *Elements of Leaders of Character* is to create more leaders of character by inspiring readers to adopt and take charge of the development of all of the elements in their own lives, then the book truly is about self-improvement. The attributes, practices, and principles are individual personal aspects; therefore, the benefits from this book will be determined by each reader in how the ideas benefit, or improve, each of us personally.

Happy successful people create their lives—everybody else is created by their lives.

Of course self-improvement is not just the domain of leaders; it is important for everyone. The self-improvement industry is a multimillion-dollar business in the United States alone. The idea, necessity, and difficulty of self-improvement has been discussed since early in mankind's history as evidenced by these quotes from Aristotle and Socrates from over two thousand years ago.

> I count him braver who overcomes his desires than
> him who conquers his enemies; for the hardest victory
> is over self.
> —Aristotle, (384-322 BC) classical Greek philosopher

> Employ your time in improving yourself by other
> men's writings, so that you shall gain easily what
> others have labored hard for.
> —Socrates, (469-399 BC) classical Greek philosopher

Self-improvement is vital as complacency and stasis are extremely detrimental to all of us. No aspect of us ever stays the same; we are either advancing or declining all the time. In fact, for humans, stasis does not exist; stasis is actually a decline because of the law of atrophy. The most important point for leaders to be aware of is if we do not continuously improve ourselves, the rest of the continuously advancing world will pass us by.

> Let us strive to improve ourselves, for we cannot
> remain stationary; one either progresses or retrogrades.
> —Marie Anne de Vichy-Chamrond, French hostess
> and patron of the arts

Self-improvement is an expansive concept considering all of the complex parts and components that we are comprised of. To simplify it somewhat, following is a listing of the major aspects that modern self-improvement focuses on.

- **Educational:** abilities, common sense, knowledge, skills, etc.
- **Emotional:** understanding and controlling emotions, companionship, love, etc.
- **Mental:** disposition, mental health, self-talk, self-view, etc.
- **Physical:** our body, diet, health maintenance, physical fitness, etc.
- **Social:** companionship, friendship, human interactions, etc.
- **Spiritual:** belief in something bigger than self, faith, morals, values, etc.

Lifetime self-improvement takes phenomenal commitment and self-discipline, but it also takes an innate and much more guttural or instinctual driving force heretofore never discussed called "want to." "Want to" is absolutely the only common element that every human being who ever accomplished anything at all shared. From the dawn of mankind, any time humanity progressed or advanced, it was because someone had the "want to" in order to make it happen. Consequently, "want to" is the foundational key to all accomplishment, happiness, and success.

One way to understand "want to" is by examining its opposite. The lack of "want to" is described by a group of several words such as inert, comfortable, complacent, unambitious, contented, indifferent, and unmotivated. Apathy and laziness are certainly mortal enemies of "want to." These antonyms might suggest that ambition, desire, drive, or motivation are synonymous for "want to;" however, these are all built upon "want to." "Want to" can exist without them, but they cannot exist without "want to." For most any significant achievement, we have got to want it first in order to ever begin, then we utilize ambition, desire, drive, or motivation, to energize us through the difficulties anything worthwhile always entails. "Want to" is the guttural drive that sustains us across all of the tidal-like ups and downs of ambition, desire, drive, or motivation.

"Want to" is the greatest force on earth, nothing can stop you if you have it—nothing!

Humans have the unique ability to derail our own lives with poor choices or lack of self-control, but we also have the unique ability to do incredible things and reach unbelievable heights of achievement. A major requirement of reaching unbelievable heights is becoming the kind of person that it takes. Becoming that kind of person requires consciously and continuously improving and developing ourselves so that we are prepared to be the kind of person that it takes to reach such lofty success. Knowing, improving, and developing self, character, and leadership ability are all definitely part of every leader's lifetime processes.

If you aim at nothing, you're guaranteed to hit what you're aiming at—whether it's shooting a gun or going through life. The problem is it's much easier to aim at nothing—there's no worry of failing or missing, but then there's no achievement either.

CHAPTER 51

Stand Out above the Crowd

Leaders of character are mandated to set the example and standard for others to follow; therefore leaders must strive to stand out from the crowd—above the crowd—in every way and element. To do this, leaders work hard to be remarkable, which simply means being noticed and talked about; being "remarked" about. The key is being noticed for the right reasons, positive reasons, by standing out above the crowd, not below. Being remarkable is an imperative for a significant impact on the world.

Being remarkable means standing out above the crowd.

The importance of being remarkable can be understood by answering the question, What are you if you are not remarkable? Unremarkable. Being unremarkable simply means blending into the crowd, being like everyone else—average or mediocre. The truth is, even being very good at something is likely unremarkable because in the modern-day focus on specialization, most of the people we are surrounded by every day are very good at what they do. The result of being unremarkable for leaders is significantly less influence and drastically less success in life and in our leadership.

Being remarkable is not terribly difficult since it seems the majority of people settle for average, blending in, or just getting by. One part of being remarkable is doing your job, and then some; fulfilling your duty, and then some; adding value to the world, and then some; giving everything you do your best effort, and then some; getting results, and then some; being responsible and disciplined, and then some. It's the "and then some" that makes us remarkable and all it has to be is one percent more than everyone else. All it takes to stand out from the crowd is doing a little more and being a person of a little stronger, more positive, and more virtuous character.

> Study while others are sleeping; work while others are
> loafing; prepare while others are playing; and dream
> while others are wishing.
> —William Arthur Ward, author, educator, and
> motivational speaker

Following are a few best practices for being remarkable:

- Display unequaled civility, friendliness, and courtesy.
- Work hard—being the hardest worker is certainly a remarkable ability today.
- Be extraverted, gregarious, and outgoing; it is a learnable skill (like it or not, those people get more attention and opportunities).
- Be liked; nothing else you do to be remarkable will matter unless people like you.
- Be audacious; showing no timidity is extremely powerful.
- Be completely trustworthy; never forget that trust is one of our most valuable assets.
- Be dependable; be someone people know they can depend on.

- Be proactive; get things done early instead of waiting until the last minute (like most others do).
- Be the first to raise your hand, the first to volunteer.
- Never meet a stranger; be able to carry on a conversation with anyone and everyone.
- Have something intelligent to talk about; know a lot about a wide breadth of topics.
- Have hobbies or interests that make for good conversation.
- Know the rules of etiquette or protocol.
- Get to know people; make friends with everyone you can.
- Remember names; the importance of being good with names cannot be overstated.
- Always be on the lookout for ways to help other people get what they want; help them be successful.
- Treat everyone like they are remarkable, no matter who they are.
- Be genuinely appreciative of others; "thank you" is just a bare minimum.
- Be a professional question asker; people like it when other people are interested in them.
- Know as much as possible about nonverbal communications and use that knowledge.

The following quotes help illustrate the value of standing out above the crowd.

> Make sure you count!
> —Major General Floyd Carpenter, USAF (retired)

The greatest use of life is to spend it for something
that will outlast it.
—William James, psychologist and philosopher

You are not here merely to make a living. You are
here to enable the world to live more amply, with
greater vision, and with a finer spirit of hope and
achievement. You are here to enrich the world. You
impoverish yourself if you forget this errand.
—Woodrow Wilson, twenty-eighth president of the
United States

The real tragedy is not being remarkable—blending into the background. Nothing great ever came from average or mediocre. In the end, significance is how our leadership, life, and legacy will be measured.

Being remarkable means being as good a leader as possible, the kind of leader others talk about for the right reasons.

CHAPTER 52

Live by an Elevated Code

Leaders of character hold themselves to a higher standard and consciously try to live their everyday lives according to an elevated code of standards. Living like that means putting character ahead of everything else. With character as the main priority, all other good, positive, and virtuous things in life will flourish. Living by an elevated code means intending to have a significant and positive impact on the world and everyone we touch, impact, or influence in any way. Living by an elevated code means expecting more from ourselves; avoiding petty, nefarious, or questionable situations; and associating with people who push us even higher.

Living by an elevated code means a leader holds his or her character, honor, and integrity as priceless.

This living by an elevated code is not a new idea, there have been other isolated groups living as such throughout history. To illustrate this concept, following are some codes from the past that illustrate several specific actions that exemplify living by a higher standard.

Gene Autry's Cowboy Code of Honor[16]

1. A cowboy never takes unfair advantage—even of an enemy.
2. A cowboy never betrays a trust. He never goes back on his word.
3. A cowboy always tells the truth.
4. A cowboy is kind and gentle to small children, old folks, and animals.
5. A cowboy is free from racial and religious intolerances.
6. A cowboy is always helpful when someone is in trouble.
7. A cowboy is always a good worker.
8. A cowboy respects womanhood, his parents, and his nation's laws.
9. A cowboy is clean about his person in thought, word, and deed.
10. A cowboy is a patriot.

The Knight's Code of Chivalry[17]

1. To fear God and maintain His Church
2. To serve the liege lord in valor and faith
3. To protect the weak and defenseless
4. To give succor to widows and orphans
5. To refrain from the wanton giving of offence
6. To live by honor and for glory
7. To despise pecuniary reward

---

[16] Codes of the West. <http://www.phantomranch.net/bwestern/creeds.htm>. Web. 19 June 2013

[17] Code of Chivalry. http://www.medieval-life-and-times.info/medieval-knights/code-of-chivalry.htm. Web. 19June 2013.

8. To fight for the welfare of all
9. To obey those placed in authority
10. To guard the honor of fellow knights
11. To eschew unfairness, meanness, and deceit
12. To keep faith
13. At all times to speak the truth
14. To persevere to the end in any enterprise begun
15. To respect the honor of women
16. Never to refuse a challenge from an equal
17. Never to turn the back upon a foe

The Leader of Character Code of Honorable Conduct

A leader of character will

- set the standard—the standard is at minimum a life of elevated honor, honesty, integrity, trustworthiness, morality, and respect for others;
- voice the standard—publicizing the standard for others to understand and follow as well; and
- live the standard—setting the example every day and in every situation for all others to adopt.

Leaders must never underestimate the incredible influential power of their example or their character.

CHAPTER 53

Conclusion
Why Such a Focus on Character

Traditional conclusions generally review and summarize the material covered in the book; however, we will part somewhat from that in order to inject a final point—perhaps the most important point in the book.

The concept of *character* has been touched on repeatedly throughout this book—the word is even in its title. What character is, what it is not, what it does, and numerous other details have entered the discussion throughout the book as well. It is obviously a very important concept, so one more question about character should be answered here in order to bring the intent of this book together: What is so important or valuable about character to me?

The short answer is this: just about every chapter, facet, and aspect of life is impacted by, controlled by, or completely determined by our character—by the kind of person we really are in our deepest recesses. Our character is the determinant of our life stories—good, bad, or ugly! The following three-word 2,500-year-old quote screams the most basic premise of the value of character, this book, and leaders of character.

Character is destiny.

—Heraclitus (535-475 BC), pre-Socratic Greek
philosopher

Heraclitus' quote illustrates a critical fact of life: our destiny is where
we end up in life, and our character will determine whatever and
wherever that is. Therefore, in order to create the destiny we wish for,
regardless of whatever that is, we simply must develop the character
that is required. We must become the kind of person we need to be in
order to end up where we wish to end up. Success is not what is most
important, becoming the kind of person it takes to become successful is
what is most important. And because character limits or magnifies our
success, the stronger and more solid our character, the greater heights
we will reach in our success, leadership, impact, happiness, and all other
aspects of our life.

> Destiny is not a matter of chance, it is a matter of
> choice; it is not a thing to be waited for, it is a thing to
> be achieved.
> —William Jennings Bryan, American populist
> politician

Character is destiny—my character is my destiny, and your character is your destiny!

> Character, in the long run, is the decisive factor in the
> life of an individual and of nations alike.
> —Theodore Roosevelt, twenty-sixth president of the
> United States

The character of society's leader's is society's destiny: hence, the critical need for leaders of character.

And that is the value of character and this book—*The Elements of Leaders of Character*—because the elements of leaders of character are the same elements of everyone's character.

Live with character; lead with character!

APPENDIX A

Helpful Leadership Books

This list of books is a treasure trove of very helpful and educational leadership and character development information. This is by no means a comprehensive list; there are many more great sources of leadership education.

- *9 Things a Leader Must Do: How to Go to the Next Level—And Take Others with You.* Henry Cloud (2006).
- *A Leader's Legacy.* Kouzes & Posner (2006).
- *ABC's of Leadership: 26 Characteristics of More Effective Leadership.* David Hall (2007).
- *Authentic Leadership: Rediscovering the Secrets to Creating Lasting Value.* Bill George (2004).
- *Be a People Person: Effective Leadership Through Effective Relationships.* John Maxwell (2007).
- *Become a Better You: 7 Keys to Improving Your Life Every Day.* Joel Osteen (2007).
- *Becoming a Person of Influence: How to Positively Impact the Lives of Others.* John Maxwell (1997).
- *Built to Last: Successful Habits of Visionary Companies.* Jim Collins & Jerry Porras (2002).

- *Business Class: Etiquette Essentials for Success at Work.* Jacqueline Whitmore (2005).
- *Change Anything: The New Science of Personal Success.* Patterson, Grenny, Maxfield, & McMillan (2012).
- *Change-Friendly Leadership: How to Transform Good Intentions into Great Performance.* R. D. Duncan & Stephen Covey (2012).
- *Charismatic Leadership: The Elusive Factor in Organizational Effectiveness.* Conger and Rabindra (1988).
- *Churchill on Leadership: Executive Success in the Face of Adversity.* Steven F. Hayward (1998).
- *Competitive Leadership: Twelve Principles for Success.* Brian Billick (2001).
- *Conversationally Speaking: Tested New Ways to Increase Your Personal and Social Effectiveness.* Alan Garner (1997).
- *Courage, The Backbone of Leadership.* Gus Lee (2006).
- *Courageous Leadership.* Bill Hybels (2002).
- *Creating Magic: 10 Common Sense Leadership Strategies from a Life at Disney.* Lee Cockerell (2008).
- *Crucial Conversation Tools for Talking When Stakes Are High.* Patterson, Grenny, McMillan, Switzler (2011).
- *Dig Your Well before You're Thirsty: The Only Networking Book You'll Ever Need.* Harvey MacKay (1999).
- *Do the Right Thing.* Mike Huckabee (2008).
- *Emily Post's Etiquette*, 18th Edition. Peggy Post (2011).
- *Emily Post's The Etiquette Advantage in Business: Personal Skills for Professional Success.* Peggy Post (2005).
- *EntreLeadership: 20 Years of Practical Business Wisdom from the Trenches.* Dave Ramsey (2011).

- *Ethics, the Heart of Leadership*, 2nd Edition. Joanne B. Ciulla (2004).
- *Everyday Leadership: Attitudes and Actions for Respect and Success (A guidebook for teens)*. Mariam G. MacGregor (2006).
- *Everything I Know about Business I Learned at McDonald's*. Paul Facella (2008).
- *Execution: The Discipline of Getting Things Done*. Bossidy & Burck (2002).
- *Fire Them Up!: 7 Simple Secrets to Inspire!: Sell Yourself with Charisma and Confidence*. Carmine Gallo (2007).
- *First, Break All the Rules: What the World's Greatest Managers Do Differently*. Marcus Buckingham & Curt Coffman (1999).
- *George Washington on Leadership*. Richard Brookhiser (2008).
- *Good to Great: Why Some Companies Make the Leap … and Others Don't*. Jim Collins (2001).
- *Greater Than Yourself: The Ultimate Lesson of True Leadership*. Steve Farber (2009).
- *Heroic Leadership: Best Practices from a 450-Year-Old Company That Changed the World*. Chris Lowney (2005).
- *How Remarkable Women Lead: The Breakthrough Model for Work and Life*. Joanna Barsh (2009).
- *How to Talk to Anyone: 92 Little Tricks for Big Success in Relationships*. Leil Lowndes (2003).
- *How to Win Friends & Influence People*. Dale Carnegie (1998).
- *In Search of Excellence: Lessons from America's Best Run Companies*. Tom Peters & Waterman (1982).
- *Influence: The Psychology of Persuasion*. Robert B. Cialdini (1993).
- *Influencer: The Power to Change Anything*. Patterson, Grenny, Maxfield, & McMillan (2007).

- *It's Your Ship.* Capt. Michael Abrashoff (2002).
- *Jack Welch and The 4 E's of Leadership: How to Put GE's Leadership Formula to Work in Your Organization.* Jeffrey Krames (2005).
- *Jesus, CEO: Using Ancient Wisdom for Visionary Leadership.* Laurie Beth Jones (1992).
- *Launching a Leadership Revolution: Mastering the Five Levels of Influence.* Chris Brady (2007).
- *Leaders Make the Future: Ten New Leadership Skills for an Uncertain World.* Bob Johansen (2012).
- *Leaders Who Last.* Dave Kraft (2010).
- *Leaders Who Make a Difference: Leadership Lessons from Three Great Bible Leaders.* Paul Chappell (2009).
- *Leaders: Strategies for Taking Charge.* Warren G. Bennis (2003).
- *Leadership.* Rudolph Giuliani (2005).
- *Leadership.* James MacGregor Burns (1978).
- *Leadership 101.* John Maxwell (2009).
- *Leadership and Self Deception: Getting out of the Box.* Arbinger Institute (2002).
- *Leadership Can Be Taught: A Bold Approach for a Complex World.* Sharon Parks (2005).
- *Leadership Code: Five Rules to Lead By.* Ulrich, Smallwood, et al. (2008).
- *Leadership Essentials: Shaping Vision, Multiplying Influence, Defining Character.* Ogden & Meyer (2007).
- *Leadership from the Inside Out: Becoming a Leader for Life.* Kevin Cashman (2008).
- *Leadership Gold.* John Maxwell (2008).
- *Leadership Is an Art.* Max Depree (2004).

- *Leadership on the Line: Staying Alive Through the Dangers of Leading.* Heifetz, Linsky, et al. (2002).
- *Leadership Secrets of Attila the Hun.* Wess Roberts (1990).
- *Leadership: A Communication Perspective.* Hackman & Johnson (2008).
- *Leadership: Theory and Practice.* Peter Guy Northouse (2012).
- *Leading Change.* John P. Kotter (1996).
- *Leading from the Front: No-Excuse Leadership Tactics for Women.* Lynch & Morgan (2006).
- *Leading with Honor: Leadership Lessons from the Hanoi Hilton.* Lee Ellis (2012).
- *Leading with the Heart: Coach K's Successful Strategies for Basketball, Business, and Life.* Mike Krzyzewski (2001).
- *Learning to Lead: A Workbook on Becoming a Leader.* Warren G. Bennis (2010).
- *Letters from Leaders: Personal Advice for Tomorrow's Leaders from the World's Most Influential People.* Henry O. Dormann (2009).
- *Lincoln on Leadership: Executive Strategies for Tough Times.* Donald T. Phillips (1993).
- *Little Black Book of Connections: 6.5 Assets for Networking Your Way to Rich Relationships.* Jeffrey Gitomer (2006).
- *Love Leadership: The New Way to Lead in a Fear-Based World.* John Hope Bryant (2009).
- *Made to Stick: Why Some Ideas Survive and Others Die.* Chip Heath (2007).
- *Management of Organizational Behavior: Leading Human Resources.* Ken Blanchard, Hersey, & Johnson (2008).
- *Man's Search for Meaning.* Viktor E. Frankl (2006).

- *Martin Luther King, Jr., on Leadership: Inspiration and Wisdom for Challenging Times.* Donald T. Phillips (2000).
- *Mastering Leadership.* Michael Williams (2006).
- *Mastering Self-Leadership: Empowering Yourself for Personal Excellence* (4th Edition). Neck and Manz (2006).
- *Monday Morning Leadership: 8 Mentoring Sessions You Can't Afford to Miss.* David Cottrell (2002).
- *Never Eat Alone: And Other Secrets to Success, One Relationship at a Time.* Keith Ferrazzi (2005).
- *Next Generation Leader: 5 Essentials for Those Who Will Shape the Future.* Andy Stanley (2006).
- *Now, Discover Your Strengths.* Marcus Buckingham & Donald O. Clifton (2001).
- *On Becoming a Leader.* Warren G. Bennis (2009).
- *Organizational Culture and Leadership*, 2nd Edition. Schein, Edgar (1992).
- *Out of Character: Surprising Truths about the Liar, Cheat, Sinner (and Saint) Lurking in All of Us.* David DeSteno & Piercarlo Valdesolo (2011).
- *Outstanding Leadership (Seconds Away from).* Molly Harvey (2011).
- *Overcoming the Five Dysfunctions of a Team: A Field Guide for Leaders, Managers and Facilitators.* Patrick M. Lencioni (2005).
- *Patton on Leadership.* Alan Axelrod (2001).
- *Primal Leadership: Realizing the Power of Emotional Intelligence.* Daniel Goleman (2004).
- *Principle Centered Leadership.* Stephen R. Covey (1992).
- *Quiet Leadership: Six Steps to Transforming Performance at Work.* David Rock (2007).

- *Remarkable Leadership: Unleashing Your Leadership Potential One Skill at a Time.* Kevin Eikenberry (2007).
- *Self-Leadership and the One-Minute Manager.* Ken Blanchard, Fowler & Hawkins (2005).
- *Servant Leadership: A Journey into the Nature of Legitimate Power and Greatness.* Robert K. Greenleaf (1977).
- *Servant Leadership: A Journey into the Nature of Legitimate Power and Greatness,* 25th Anniversary Edition. Robert K. Greenleaf (2002).
- *Seven Lessons for Leading in Crisis.* Bill George (2009).
- *Start with Why.* Simon Sinek (2011).
- *Steve Jobs: Ten Lessons in Leadership.* Michael Essany (2012).
- *Still Surprised: A Memoir of a Life in Leadership.* Warren G. Bennis (2010).
- *Strengths-Based Leadership.* Tom Rath (2009).
- *Switch: How to Change Things When Change Is Hard.* Chip & Dan Heath (2010).
- *Talent Is Never Enough.* John Maxwell (2007).
- *The 17 Indisputable Laws of Teamwork: Embrace Them and Empower Your Team.* John Maxwell (2001).
- *The 21 Indispensable Qualities of a Leader.* John Maxwell (1999).
- *The 21 Irrefutable Laws of Leadership: Follow Them and People Will Follow You.* John Maxwell (2007).
- *The 360-Degree Leader: Developing Your Influence from Anywhere in the Organization.* John Maxwell (2006).
- *The 5 Levels of Leadership: Proven Steps to Maximize Your Potential.* John Maxwell (2011).
- *The 7 Habits of Highly Effective People.* Stephen R. Covey (2004).

- *The 8th Habit.* Stephen R. Covey (2005).
- *The Architecture of Leadership: Preparation Equals Performance.* Donald T. Phillips & Adm. James M. Loy (2008).
- *The Art of Mingling: Proven Techniques for Mastering Any Room.* Jeanne Martinet (2006).
- *The Book of Virtues.* William Bennett (1993).
- *The Charismatic Leader.* Jay A. Conger (1989).
- *The Difference Maker: Making Your Attitude Your Greatest Asset.* John Maxwell (2006).
- *The Energy Bus: 10 Rules to Fuel Your Life, Work, and Team with Positive Energy.* Jon Gordon (2007).
- *The Fifth Discipline: The Art and Practice of the Learning Organization.* Peter M. Senge (1990).
- *The Fine Art of Small Talk: How to Start a Conversation, Keep It Going, Build Networking Skills.* Debra Fine (2005).
- *The Five Dysfunctions of a Team: A Leadership Fable.* Patrick M. Lencioni (2002).
- *The Founding Fathers on Leadership: Classic Teamwork in Changing Times.* Donald T. Phillips (1998).
- *The Future of Leadership.* Bennis, Spreitzer & Cummings (2001).
- *The Game-Changer: How You Can Drive Revenue and Profit Growth with Innovation.* A. G. Lafley & Ram Charan (2008).
- *The Introverted Leader: Building on Your Quiet Strength.* Jennifer B. Kahnweiler (2009).
- *The Introvert's Guide to Success in Business and Leadership.* Lisa Petrilli (2011).
- *The Last Lecture.* Randy Pausch (2008).
- *The Leader Who Had No Title—A Modern Fable on Real Success in Business and Life.* Robin Sharma (2010).

- *The Leadership Advantage: How the Best Companies Are Developing Their Talent to Pave the Way for Future Success.* Robert M. Fulmer (2008).
- *The Leadership Challenge.* Kouzes & Posner (1995).
- *The Leadership Secrets of Santa Claus.* Harvey & Cottrell (2003).
- *The One-Minute Manager.* Ken Blanchard & Spencer Johnson (1981).
- *The Right Thing.* Scott Waddle (2003).
- *The Secret Language of Leadership: How Leaders Inspire Action Through Narrative.* Stephen Denning (2007).
- *The Secret: What Great Leaders Know and Do.* Ken Blanchard (2009).
- *The Small Talk Handbook: Easy Instructions on How to Make Small Talk in Any Situation.* Melissa Wadsworth (2012).
- *The Ten Commandments of Character: Essential Advice for Living an Honorable, Ethical, Honest Life.* Joseph Telushkin (2003).
- *The Tipping Point: How Little Things Can Make a Big Difference.* Malcolm Gladwell (2002).
- *The Trusted Leader.* Robert M. Galford (2002).
- *The Truth about Leadership: The No-fads, Heart-of-the-Matter Facts You Need to Know.* Kouzes & Posner (2010).
- *The Winning Attitude.* John Maxwell (2008).
- *Theodore Roosevelt on Leadership: Executive Lessons from the Bully Pulpit.* James M. Strock (2001).
- *Total Leadership: Be a Better Leader, Have a Richer Life.* Stewart D. Friedman (2008).
- *Tribal Leadership: Leveraging Natural Groups to Build a Thriving Organization.* Logan, King, et al. (2008).
- *Tribes: We Need You to Lead Us.* Seth Godin (2008).

- *True North: Discover Your Authentic Leadership.* Bill George & Peter Sims (2007).
- *Ultimate Leadership: Winning Execution Strategies for Your Situation.* Russell Palmer (2008).
- *Uncommon Leadership: Servant Leadership in a Power-Based World*, 2nd Edition. Robert D. Kuest (2009).
- *Unusually Excellent: The Necessary Nine Skills Required for the Practice of Great Leadership.* John Hamm (2011).
- *Visioneering: God's Blueprint for Developing and Maintaining Personal Vision.* Andy Stanley (2005).
- *What Got You Here Won't Get You There.* Marshal Goldsmith (2007).
- *What Leaders Really Do.* John P. Kotter (1999).
- *Where Have All the Leaders Gone.* Lee Iacocca (2008).
- *Who Moved My Cheese?* Spencer Johnson (1998).
- *Win the Crowd: Unlock the Secrets of Influence, Charisma, and Showmanship.* Steve Cohen (2006).
- *Wit and Wisdom of General George S. Patton: Laws of Leadership Series*, Volume VI. Charlie Jones (2007).
- *Wooden on Leadership.* John Wooden (2005).
- *You Don't Need a Title to Be a Leader: How Anyone, Anywhere, Can Make a Positive Difference.* Mark Sanborn (2006).

APPENDIX B

Potential Values

After reading the values chapter so that you have a clear understanding of values, to begin defining your values, scan through this entire list and note each word that resonates with you and words that you know are important to you. When you are finished, go back through and choose the top ten or twelve of the words you chose. These are a good representation of your values.

Abundance	Affection
Acceptance	Affluence
Accessibility	Aggressiveness
Accomplishment	Agility
Accountability	Alertness
Accuracy	Altruism
Achievement	Ambition
Acknowledgment	Amusement
Activeness	Anticipation
Adaptability	Appreciation
Adoration	Approachability
Adroitness	Approval
Advancement	Artistic talent
Adventure	Assertiveness

Attentiveness

Attractiveness

Audacity

Availability

Awareness

Awe

Balance

Beauty

Being the best

Belonging

Benevolence

Bliss

Boldness

Bravery

Breaking rules

Brilliance

Calmness

Camaraderie

Candor

Capability

Care

Carefulness

Celebrity

Certainty

Challenge

Character

Charity

Charm

Chastity

Cheerfulness

Chivalry

Clarity

Cleanliness

Clear-mindedness

Cleverness

Closeness

Charisma

Commitment

Community

Compassion

Competence

Competition

Composure

Concentration

Confidence

Conformity

Congruency

Connection

Consciousness

Consensus

Conservation

Consistency

Contentment

Continuity

Contribution

Control

Conversation

Conviction

Coolness

Cooperation

Cordiality	Duty
Correctness	Dynamism
Courage	Eagerness
Courtesy	Economy
Craftiness	Ecstasy
Creativity	Education
Credibility	Effectiveness
Cunning	Efficiency
Curiosity	Elation
Daring	Elegance
Decisiveness	Empathy
Decorum	Encouragement
Delight	Endurance
Democracy	Energy
Dependability	Enjoyment
Depth	Entertainment
Desire	Enthusiasm
Determination	Environmentalism
Devotion	Ethics
Devoutness	Etiquette
Dignity	Excellence
Diligence	Excitement
Directness	Exhilaration
Discipline	Expectancy
Discovery	Expediency
Discretion	Experience
Diversity	Expertise
Dominance	Exploration
Dreaming	Expressiveness
Drive	Extravagance

Extroversion	Guidance
Exuberance	Guts
Fairness	Happiness
Faith	Harmony
Fame	Health
Fascination	Heart
Fashion	Helpfulness
Fearlessness	Heroism
Ferocity	Holiness
Fidelity	Honesty
Fierceness	Honor
Financial independence	Hopefulness
Firmness	Hospitality
Fitness	Humility
Flexibility	Humor
Focus	Imagination
Fortitude	Impact
Frankness	Impartiality
Free spiritedness	Inclusion
Freedom	Independence
Friendliness	Individuality
Friendship	Industry
Frugality	Influence
Gallantry	Ingenuity
Generosity	Inquisitiveness
Giving	Insightfulness
Grace	Inspiration
Gratitude	Integrity
Gregariousness	Intellect
Growth	Intelligence

Intensity

Intimacy

Intrepidness

Introversion

Intuition

Intuitiveness

Inventiveness

Investing

Involvement

Joy

Judiciousness

Justice

Keenness

Kindness

Knowledge

Laughter

Leadership

Learning

Liberty

Liveliness

Logic

Longevity

Loyalty

Majesty

Making a difference

Manners

Marriage

Mastery

Maturity

Meaning

Meekness

Mellowness

Meticulousness

Mindfulness

Modesty

Morality

Morals

Motivation

Mysteriousness

Nature

Neatness

Nerve

Nonconformity

Obedience

Open-mindedness

Openness

Optimism

Order

Organization

Originality

Outdoors

Outlandishness

Outrageousness

Passion

Patience

Peace

Perceptiveness

Perfection

Perkiness

Perseverance

Persistence

Persuasiveness

Philanthropy

Piety

Playfulness

Pleasantness

Poise

Polish

Popularity

Practicality

Pragmatism

Precision

Preparedness

Presence

Pride

Privacy

Proactivity

Professionalism

Prosperity

Prudence

Punctuality

Purity

Rationality

Realism

Reason

Reasonableness

Recognition

Recreation

Refinement

Reflection

Relationships

Relaxation

Reliability

Religiousness

Reputation

Resilience

Resolution

Resolve

Resourcefulness

Respect

Responsibility

Rest

Restraint

Reverence

Richness

Right attitude

Rigor

Sacredness

Sacrifice

Saintliness

Satisfaction

Science

Security

Self-control

Selflessness

Self-reliance

Self-respect

Sensitivity

Sensuality

Serenity

Service	Sympathy
Sense of humor	Synergy
Sharing	Teaching
Shrewdness	Teamwork
Significance	Temperance
Silence	Thankfulness
Silliness	Thoroughness
Simplicity	Thoughtfulness
Sincerity	Thrift
Skillfulness	Tidiness
Solidarity	Timeliness
Solitude	Traditionalism
Sophistication	Tranquility
Soundness	Trust
Speed	Trustworthiness
Spirit	Truth
Spirituality	Understanding
Spontaneity	Unflappability
Spunk	Uniqueness
Stability	Unity
Status	Usefulness
Stealth	Utility
Stillness	Valor
Strength	Variety
Structure	Victory
Success	Vigor
Succinctness	Virtue
Support	Vision
Supremacy	Vitality
Surprise	Vivacity

Volunteering

Warm-heartedness

Warmth

Watchfulness

Wealth

Willfulness

Willingness

Winning

Wisdom

Wittiness

Wonder

Working alone

Working with others

Youthfulness

Zeal

APPENDIX C

Element Discussion/Reflection Questions

The following questions are offered as a learning/understanding tool. The elements can be better understood through answering and discussing the questions.

Attitude

1. Have you ever known anyone with a perpetually negative attitude? Describe that person.
2. Why do you think a positive attitude is so contagious?
3. Have you ever tried to change your attitude? How did it go?
4. Describe what you think is the right attitude for leaders of character.

Authenticity

1. Think of someone you consider to be authentic. Describe what it is that makes him or her authentic.
2. Think of someone you think is not authentic—think of a fake. Describe what it is that makes him or her not authentic.
3. Why is it, in your opinion, that neither lies nor inauthentic people can withstand the test of time? What does that mean?
4. What does calling our authenticity our "legitimacy" mean to you?

Behavior

1. Describe some behaviors that you think would not be consistent with what's expected of a leader of character. In other words, what are some things we probably should not do as leaders of character?
2. Describe a situation exemplifying the fact that we are judged by our actions, not our intentions.
3. Do you believe the idea that one bad or stupid decision could derail our entire life? Why?
4. Why do you think our behavior is such a powerful influencer?

Charisma

1. Describe your idea of what charisma is.
2. Do you know someone who is very charismatic? Describe him/her.
3. Do you think charisma is valuable to leaders? Why or why not?
4. Do you think charisma is a learnable skill? Why or why not?

Commitment

1. What are you committed to? Why?
2. List some things that probably don't deserve your commitment. Why?
3. Why do you think commitment is so rare in America?
4. Why do you think that if the leader isn't committed, nobody is?

Communication Skills

1. Why do you think so many people suffer with poor communication skills?
2. What does truly listening with eyes, ears, body language, and mind tell the person we are communicating with?
3. How do you think you can develop emotional awareness?

4. Have you ever given a formal speech to a large group? Were you scared? How did you overcome your fear? What advice would you give someone about to give his or her first speech?

Compassion

1. Who is the most compassionate person you know? Describe him/her and his/her compassion.
2. List several examples of compassionate acts you've witnessed or been party to.
3. Do you think some people are more capable of compassion than others? Why?
4. Do you think compassion has any importance to nonleaders? Why?

Competence

1. Think of someone you consider very competent. Describe what it is about him or her that makes them so competent.
2. Have you ever witnessed incompetence? Describe it.
3. List ten roles you play in life. Describe how you develop competence in each of those roles.
4. Have you ever experienced your intuition or instinct? Describe it.

Confidence

1. Describe your idea of confidence.
2. Think of someone you know who seems to be very self-confident. Describe what makes you think he or she is so self-confident.
3. Do you think confidence is situational (depends on the situation)? Explain.
4. What do you think is the one best way to develop confidence?

Courage

1. Why do you think we humans are so afraid of humiliation or ridicule?
2. Think about someone you know who is courageous. Describe what it is about him or her that makes you think he or she is courageous.
3. Describe an incident when you stepped up and made a mistake or failed.
4. Describe an example of the contagiousness of courage.

Creativity

1. Do you consider yourself to be creative? Why or why not? Do you think people are genetically (born) creative?
2. What do you think "leadership is about change and creativity is required to drive change in the right direction" means?
3. What do you think Erich Fromm meant by, "Creativity requires the courage to let go of certainties"?
4. Do you think creativity can be taught and learned?

Credibility

1. Do you think you have credibility? Explain.
2. Who is the most credible person you know? What makes him/her the most credible?
3. List ten things that you think would destroy credibility.
4. Have you ever been witness to anyone losing credibility? Explain.

Discipline

1. Do you know anyone who is undisciplined? Describe him or her.
2. Think about yourself. You have some discipline or you wouldn't be reading this book, so describe your discipline. What do you do that takes discipline?

3. Still thinking about yourself and your discipline, what would happen to your life if you lost all of your discipline?

4. What about your life would improve if you improved your discipline?

Flexibility/Adaptability

1. Describe a time when you had to be flexible.

2. Have you ever been held accountable when you did not want to be? Explain.

3. Why do you think people are so resistant to change?

4. Have you ever been forced to change or know someone who has? Describe it.

Honesty

1. Have you ever known a liar? Describe how you know he or she was a liar.

2. Have you ever known someone who was an obvious cheater? What made him or her obvious? Describe him or her.

3. Describe how you might answer a question that the honest answer would be hurtful to the person asking the question.

4. Why do you think you would sacrifice your trustworthiness, respect, and credibility if you sacrifice your honesty? What have they got to do with each other?

Honor

1. Describe honor in your own words.

2. If you've had any connection to the military, describe military honor.

3. Why do you think honor is so inherent in the military?

4. What do you think is so valuable about honor for leaders of character?

Humility

1. Describe the most humble person you have ever known.
2. Describe the most arrogant person you have ever known.
3. What do you think St. Augustine meant by this: "Humility is the foundation of all the other virtues hence, in the soul in which this virtue does not exist there cannot be any other virtue except in mere appearance"?
4. How does pride make us artificial and humility make us real?

Integrity

1. Describe integrity in your own words.
2. Do you have integrity? What makes you answer that way?
3. Think of someone who doesn't have integrity. Describe that person.
4. Why do you think that if we sacrifice our integrity, we can never fully regain it?

Intuition

1. Describe intuition. Do you have it?
2. Do you think women have better intuition than men? Explain.
3. What do you think Einstein meant by, "The only real valuable thing is intuition"?
4. Do you think intuition can be developed or learned? Why or why not?

Knowledge

1. What do you do to develop knowledge?
2. Why do you think developing knowledge is the key to a long life?

3. What do you think the concept of lifelong learning really means?
4. Why do you think, as leaders, we must have a wide range of knowledge?

Locus of Control
1. What is your locus of control? Explain.
2. Why do you think most great leaders and successful people had an internal locus of control?
3. Do you or anyone you know have an external locus of control? Describe it or them.
4. What do you think Henry Ford meant by, "If you think you can do it, or you think you can't do it, you are right"?

Morality and Ethics
1. Have you ever been witness to an unethical act? Describe it.
2. Do you think the concept of our moral fabric is viable and real? Why or why not?
3. Why do you think usually moral people sometimes do unethical things?
4. Describe a positive experience you've had with your moral compass when it led you in the right direction. Describe an experience when it didn't.

Optimism
1. What do you think the main advantage of optimism is? Why?
2. Have you ever known a pessimist? Describe them.
3. What do you think "optimism and hope are jet fuel for our capabilities" means?
4. What do you think "optimism is a leader's influence multiplier" means?

Passion

1. Describe passion in your own words.
2. Think of someone you think of as passionate. Describe what it is about him or her that makes you think of them as passionate.
3. Do you think some people are naturally more passionate about life in general, so they're naturally more passionate about other things as well?
4. Are you passionate about anything? What? Were you born passionate about it or did you develop that passion?

People Skills

1. In what area could you improve your people skills?
2. What do you think about networking? Is it important?
3. Do you think it is important to know a lot of people, or have a lot of people know you? Why?
4. Do you think the people with great people skills were born with them or did they develop them?

Perseverance

1. Describe your work ethic. How could you improve your work ethic?
2. Do you think you could be one of the best in the world at something if you had the perseverance and commitment to doing what you had to do to reach that point?
3. Have you ever had a situation where perseverance was required? Describe it.
4. What do you think Emerson meant in the quote, "Good luck is another name for tenacity of purpose"? What has luck got to do with perseverance?

Professionalism

1. Do you think about the way you dress and what impact it might have on your life? Explain why.
2. Do you believe guilt by association is true? Explain why.
3. What do you think Emily Post meant by, "Etiquette is the science of living. It embraces everything. It is ethics. It is honor"?
4. What do you think James Garfield meant when he said, "If the power to do hard work is not a skill, it's the best possible substitute for it"?

Respect

1. Describe disrespect.
2. Have you ever had a boss or leader who did not respect you? Explain.
3. Describe how your leadership might be affected if you were not respected.
4. Describe several ways to give respect so that others know you respect them.

Responsibility/Accountability

1. Do you know anyone who is irresponsible? Describe his/her irresponsibility.
2. Do you know anyone who has an external locus of control? Someone who always has someone or something to blame for all his/her problems? Describe him/her.
3. What kind of person are you, an internal or external locus of control person? What makes you think that?
4. Do you make excuses for not getting things done on time or for mistakes you make? Why?

Sacrifice

1. What are some things you believe would help develop sacrifice?
2. Do you sacrifice in your daily life? Describe it.
3. Have you ever felt gratitude? Describe it.
4. How much ambition do you have? Do you think ambition is a good thing? Why?

Sense of Humor

1. Describe your sense of humor. Do you think it's important to you?
2. What do you think is the most important advantage to having a good sense of humor?
3. Can you name any instances where a sense of humor is not warranted?
4. What do you think Samuel Coleridge meant by, "No mind is thoroughly well organized that is deficient in a sense of humor"?

Trustworthiness

1. Do you know anyone who is not trustworthy? What makes them that way?
2. Has anyone ever violated your trust in them? What did it feel like?
3. Have you ever violated someone's trust in you? What did that feel like?
4. Do you believe this statement: "Once we sacrifice trust in any relationship, we will never, no matter what we do, build trust back to its presacrificed level"? Why?

Values

1. Do you think many people know what their values are?
2. Do you know what your top values are?

3. Have you ever done something that went against your values? What did it feel like?

4. Have you ever thought about how you made some of the major decisions in your life? Describe it.

Vision

1. Describe one of your personal visions.

2. Have you ever been a part of an organization that had a clear vision? Describe it.

3. Can you describe Walt Disney's vision?

4. Do you think the ability to create vision is rare? Why?

Willingness to Lead

1. Describe what your idea of willingness to lead looks like.

2. Are you a doer? Do you know any doers? Describe doers.

3. Describe what it means to "step up and lead."

4. Why do you think one of the major duties of leaders is to prepare other leaders, and even our own replacements?

CPSIA information can be obtained at www.ICGtesting.com
Printed in the USA
BVOW03s1206180314

348009BV00002B/4/P